Southern

Church Suppers

*Recipes Shared
by Church Folks*
from

Virginia

Georgia

Alabama

Arkansas

Kentucky

Louisiana

Tennessee

Mississippi

South Carolina

North Carolina

9   8   7   6   5   4   3   2   1

ISBN 978-1-889593-16-6
PUBLISHED BY:
3D Press, Inc.
a Big Earth Publishing company
3005 Center Green Drive, Suite 220
Boulder, CO 80301

800-258-5830 (order toll free)
303-443-9687 (fax)
www.bigearthpublishing.com

COVER AND TEXT DESIGN: Rebecca Finkel
EDITING: Claire Summerfield
PRINTED IN China by Imago

Contents

> *Long before institutionalized religions*
> *came along—and temples and churches—*
> *there was an unquestioned recognition*
> *that what goes on in the kitchen is holy.*
> *Cooking involves an enormously rich coming-together*
> *of the fruits of the earth with the inventive genius*
> *of the human being.*
>
> —LAUREL ROBERTSON

Introduction

Welcome to the world of legendary Southern-style cook-ing with recipes kindly provided by church folks in ten Southern states. Church-going members of our society are often quite experienced chefs in their community. A lifetime of supply-ing food for church potlucks, picnics, weddings, funerals, baptisms, christenings, as well as respite meals for those in need, offers plenty of opportunities to practice culinary skills. It is common for those in attendance at a church potluck supper to seek out a particular parishioner's specialty dish: the freshest deviled eggs, tastiest cheese sticks, most delicious potato salad, crispiest fried chicken, spiciest barbequed ribs, creamiest macaroni and cheese, fluffiest biscuits, or the most delectable coconut cake. All of the recipes in *Southern Church Suppers* were submitted by seasoned veterans of this natural selection process for the best foodstuffs in their church community.

Long before the majority of Southerners were concentrated in urban areas, life on widespread plantations was the norm. Neighbors were few and far between. The community church was not only the focal point for worship on Sunday, but also the primary outlet for social interaction. Due to the distance and mode of transpor-tation from plantation to church, communal Sunday suppers were an opportunity for continued fellowship during the midday repast of the all-day church service. Good food was an essential element, both for sustenance and pleasure. Huge hampers of homemade delicacies were prepared, such as pigsfoot jelly and sausage cured in cornhusks, for this midday meal enjoyed under the trees by church folk throughout the South.

In the early to mid-twentieth century, childhood memories of special Sunday suppers at home after church contained poignant flavors and sweet nostalgia. Biscuits so light they could float off the plate, fall-apart tender pot roast crowned with soft caramelized vegetables—that's what Sunday suppers were made of. It is often the quiet meals with family that contribute significant flavor to the history of our lives. Alas, this blissful time is also past.

Today, churches are creatively reclaiming community. Those seeking cultural relevance realize that technology fuels relational hunger. Community-rich events sponsored by various denominations provide a vehicle for individuals, families, and groups to meet and develop personal and spiritual connections. The company of like-minded people, along with good food, creates a mighty welcoming and sustaining environment in today's fragmented and fast-paced society.

Containing over 300 recipes, *Southern Church Suppers* covers several generations of the preferred flavors, culinary trends, and techniques representative of fabled Southern-style cooking. *Southern Church Suppers* will expose you to new food combinations or enable you to go back in time and recreate meals that are a pleasant, but faint, memory. There are recipes for the old-timey concoctions of Brunswick stew and hushpuppies, and the food-evoking memories of mom, such as Southern fried chicken and ambrosia. There are also recipes using preferably fresh and primarily organic ingredients including whole earth salad, fettuccine with crawfish and asparagus tips, and grilled white fish in lemon sauce—all with a southern twist. And to continue the tradition of cooking for a congregation, we've included several recipes that serve fifty to one hundred people.

The emphasis of *Southern Church Suppers* is on fresh flavors reflecting both urban and rural styles. Enjoy the snippets of history, wise words, anecdotes, and tiny tales that accompany the recipes. *Southern Church Suppers* is a cookbook to celebrate the significance of food and food traditions in your own family and community—no matter where your locale.

Appetizers

Food is a subject of conversation
more spiritually refreshing
even than the weather,
for the number of possible remarks
about the weather is limited,
whereas of food you can talk
on and on and on.

—A. A. MILNE

Hot Pecan Dip

Makes 2½ Cups

1 (8-ounce) package cream cheese, softened
2 tablespoons milk
½ cup sour cream
¼ cup green pepper, chopped
1 small onion, minced
½ teaspoon garlic salt
1 (2½-ounce) jar dried beef, chopped
2 tablespoons butter
½ cup pecans, coarsely chopped
½ teaspoon salt
Crackers, for serving

Preheat oven to 350°F. In a medium bowl, blend cream cheese, milk, and sour cream. Add green pepper, minced onion, garlic salt, and dried beef; stir to combine. Place mixture in 8-inch pie plate and set aside. In a small pan, melt butter, and add pecans and salt. Spread pecan mixture over cheese mixture in pie plate. Bake for 30 minutes or until light brown. Serve warm with crackers.

—*Wyonnie,* GEORGIA

Tempting Shrimp Dip

Makes 4 Cups

½ cup butter, softened
1 (8-ounce) package cream cheese, softened
2 teaspoons mayonnaise
Dash garlic powder
⅛ teaspoon pepper
⅛ teaspoon Worcestershire sauce
2 teaspoons lemon juice
1 small onion, chopped
½ cup celery, chopped
9 ounces shrimp, cooked, peeled, and chopped

In a large bowl, combine butter, cream cheese, mayonnaise, garlic powder, pepper, Worcestershire sauce, and lemon juice. Mix well. Add onion, celery, and shrimp; stir. Refrigerate for 3–4 hours before serving. —*Sally*, GEORGIA

Clam Dip

Makes 2½ Cups

1 (8-ounce) package cream cheese, softened
1 cup sour cream
1 (6½-ounce) can minced clams;
    drain and reserve clam juice
2 teaspoons lemon juice
1½ teaspoons Worcestershire sauce
½ teaspoon Lawry's Seasoned Salt™
Dash Lawry's Seasoned Pepper™
Crisp, raw vegetables, for serving

In a medium bowl, blend cream cheese and sour cream. Add clams and 1 tablespoon of reserved clam juice to the cream mixture. Add lemon juice, Worcestershire sauce, seasoned salt, and seasoned pepper; blend well. For a thinner dip, add more clam juice. Serve with crisp, raw vegetables. —*Colleen*, NORTH CAROLINA

Horseradish Bacon Dip

Makes 2½ Cups

2 cups Cheddar cheese, shredded
1 cup sour cream
¼ cup bacon, cooked and crumbled
2 tablespoons horseradish sauce
2 tablespoons chives, chopped
Crackers and sliced fresh vegetables, for serving

Place cheese, sour cream, bacon, and horseradish sauce in a blender or food processor; cover and process until smooth. Pour into a large bowl and stir in chives. Refrigerate at least 1 hour to allow flavors to blend. Serve as a dip with crackers and fresh vegetables.

—*Phyllis,* VIRGINIA

Hot Crawfish Dip 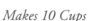 *For a Crowd*

Makes 10 Cups

½ stick (¼ cup) margarine
3 (8-ounce) packages cream cheese
1 pound Velveeta™ cheese
2 pounds crawfish tails, chopped
2 tablespoons garlic, minced
2 tablespoons Worcestershire sauce
2 tablespoons parsley flakes
1 teaspoon Old Bay Seasoning™
1 teaspoon garlic salt
Tostados™ for serving

In a large skillet, melt margarine over medium heat. Add the cream cheese and Velveeta™ and stir until melted. Add the crawfish tails and the next 5 ingredients; mix well. Serve with Tostados.™

—*Denice,* MISSISSIPPI

Shoepeg Corn Dip

Makes 5 Cups

8 ounces mayonnaise
8 ounces sour cream
2 (11-ounce) cans shoepeg corn, drained
8–10 ounces sharp Cheddar cheese, finely shredded
Chopped jalapeños, to taste

In a large bowl, mix all ingredients; cover and refrigerate.

—*Carol*, MISSISSIPPI

Shoepeg corn is the heirloom variety of white corn valued for its sweet milky flavor. The small, narrow kernels form uneven rows on the cob. In the 1800s, the term "shoepeg" was coined to describe this maize variety because the corn kernels resembled the wooden pegs used by shoemakers to attach soles to the tops of the shoes.

If you have some shoepeg corn left over after making the shoepeg corn dip featured on this page, parboil the corn, dye it, and use it for fish bait. It will stay on the hook and never get mushy. The fish love it!

Shrimp Log

Makes 6 Servings

1 (8-ounce) package cream cheese, softened
1 cup shrimp, cooked, peeled, and minced
2 tablespoons chili sauce
2 tablespoons pimento-stuffed olives, chopped
2 tablespoons green onions, chopped
1 teaspoon lemon juice
Sliced pimento-stuffed olives, for garnish
Wheat crackers, for serving

In a large bowl, stir the cream cheese until smooth. Add cooked shrimp, chili sauce, chopped olives, onion, and lemon juice; mix well. Shape into a log, place on cookie sheet, and garnish with sliced stuffed olives. Cover and chill. To serve, spread on wheat crackers.

—*Fay*, ALABAMA

Pimento Cheese Spread

Makes 2½ Cups

16 ounces sharp Cheddar cheese, softened
1 (4-ounce) jar pimentos, diced
1 teaspoon sugar
1 teaspoon vinegar
Dash ground red pepper
Dash salt
Margarine, for softening mixture

Mix first 6 ingredients. Add margarine to soften cheese to desired consistency. Refrigerate.

—*Dail*, NORTH CAROLINA

Tennessee Caviar

Makes 24 Servings

4 (15-ounce) cans black-eyed peas, drained
1 (16-ounce) can diced tomatoes with garlic and herbs
1 (15-ounce) can hominy, drained
1 (8-ounce) bottle Italian dressing
1 bunch green onions, chopped
1 green pepper, chopped
Lemon pepper, to taste
Ground red pepper, to taste
Potato chips, for serving

In a large bowl, combine first 8 ingredients. Cover and refrigerate. Serve with your favorite chips.

—*Rena*, TENNESSEE

Black-Eyed Pea Salsa

Makes 10 Cups

6 cups black-eyed peas, firmly cooked
2 cups Italian or vinaigrette salad dressing
1 cup green bell pepper, diced
1 cup red bell pepper, diced
1 cup onion, finely chopped
3–4 hot peppers, finely chopped
2 cloves garlic, pressed
1/3 cup parsley or cilantro, chopped
Pita triangles, for serving

In a large bowl, mix first 8 ingredients. Cover and refrigerate for 24 hours. Serve with pita triangles.

—*Dana*, ALABAMA

Duck Paté

For a Crowd

Makes 24 Servings

3 large wild ducks, (about 6 pounds), cleaned
3 stalks celery, cut into 2-inch pieces
1 onion, sliced
1½ teaspoons salt
¼ teaspoon pepper
4 stalks of celery, cut into 1-inch pieces
4 green onions, cut into 1-inch pieces
1 green pepper, coarsely chopped
2 tablespoons lemon juice
1 tablespoon Worcestershire sauce
¾ teaspoon salt
¼ teaspoon hot sauce
½ cup mayonnaise
Wheat crackers, for serving

In a large Dutch oven, combine the first 5 ingredients; cover with water, and bring to a boil. Reduce heat; cover and simmer for about 1 hour or until ducks are tender. Remove ducks from stock; cool, and remove meat from bones.

In a meat grinder or food processor, grind meat, 1-inch celery pieces, green onions, and green pepper. In a large bowl, combine meat mixture, lemon juice, Worcestershire sauce, salt, hot sauce, and mayonnaise; stir. Spoon into a 1-quart mold and pack lightly. Chill 3–4 hours or overnight. Remove from mold and garnish as desired. Serve with wheat crackers.

—*Wilma Jane,* ARKANSAS

Baked Gouda with Apricot

Makes 8 Servings

1 sheet frozen puff pastry, thawed
1 pound round Gouda cheese, waxed coating removed
2 tablespoons apricot preserves
1 egg white
Green apples, sliced, for serving

Preheat oven to 400°F. On waxed paper, roll out pastry until it is large enough to wrap around cheese. Spread preserves in middle of dough, and place cheese on top of preserves. Fold pastry sides up and over top of cheese, pinching edges to seal. Place the seamed side of the dough down on a parchment paper–lined baking sheet. Brush top and sides of dough with a light coat of egg white. Bake for 10 minutes. Reduce temperature to 325°F and bake until golden, about 20 minutes longer. Let stand at room temperature for 10 minutes. Cut and serve with sliced green apples. Always a party hit!

—Mary, ALABAMA

Country Ham Balls

For a Crowd

Makes 36 Small Ham Balls

3 cups Bisquick™
1½ cups country ham, cooked and chopped
4 cups Cheddar cheese, shredded
½ cup Parmesan cheese, grated
2 tablespoons parsley flakes
²/₃ cup milk

Preheat oven to 350°F. In a large bowl, combine all ingredients and mix well. Roll into 1-inch balls. Arrange in a single layer on a lightly greased baking sheet. Bake for 20–25 minutes.

—Julie, TENNESSEE

Chinese Meatballs

Makes 124 Small Meatballs

MEATBALLS:
2 pounds regular pork sausage
2 pounds hot pork sausage
1 large onion, finely chopped
4 eggs, beaten
2 cups breadcrumbs
¼ cup soy sauce

SAUCE:
½ cup cornstarch
1 cup cold water
1 cup vinegar
2 cups pineapple juice
2 cups beef consommé
¾ cup brown sugar
¼ cup soy sauce
3 tablespoons fresh ginger, grated,
     or 5 teaspoons ground ginger

Meatballs: In a large bowl, mix the 6 meatball ingredients and refrigerate. When chilled, form into 1-inch meatballs and place in a skillet. Cook on medium heat, turning as needed until cooked through.

Sauce: In a small bowl, combine cornstarch and cold water; set aside. In a large saucepan over medium heat, mix vinegar, pineapple juice, beef consommé, brown sugar, soy sauce, and ginger. Stir in the cornstarch and water mixture until sauce is thick and clear. Place meatballs in a chafing dish and pour sauce over the meatballs.

—*Roberta*, ALABAMA

Baked Crab Ragoons

For a Crowd

Makes 30 Crab Ragoons

1 medium egg white
1 (8-ounce) package cream cheese, softened
7 ounces crabmeat
1 teaspoon fresh ginger, grated
1 medium garlic clove, minced
1 teaspoon soy sauce
1 tablespoon fresh cilantro, minced (optional)
30 wonton wrappers
Non-stick cooking spray

Preheat oven to 375°F. In a large bowl, blend egg white and cream cheese. Stir in the crabmeat, ginger, minced garlic, and soy sauce. Add fresh cilantro, if desired. Spoon 2 teaspoons of the filling into each of the wonton wrappers. Lightly moisten the edges of each wonton wrapper with water. Pull up the corners and twist, forming a small bundle. Place the bundles on a large baking sheet. Spray the bundles with the non-stick cooking spray. Bake for 8–10 minutes or until lightly browned and crisp. Bundles may be deep fried instead of baked, if desired.

—*Josh*, VIRGINIA

Basic Deviled Eggs

Makes 12 Deviled Eggs

6 large eggs
2 tablespoons mayonnaise
1½ tablespoons sweet pickle relish
1 teaspoon prepared mustard
⅛ teaspoon salt
Dash of pepper
Paprika, for garnish

Place eggs in a single layer in a saucepan. Add water to the depth of 3 inches. Bring to a boil. Cover and remove from heat; let stand for 15 minutes. Drain immediately and fill the saucepan with cold water to cool the eggs. Peel eggs under cold running water. Slice eggs in half lengthwise and carefully remove yolks. Mash yolks with mayonnaise. Add relish, mustard, salt, and pepper. Stir well. Spoon yolk mixture onto egg whites. Garnish with paprika, if desired. Keep refrigerated until served.

—*Arthur*, GEORGIA

A boiled egg
raised its little lid
and revealed
its buttercup yolk.

—COLETTE

Mexican Deviled Eggs

Makes 24 Deviled Eggs

12 eggs, hard-boiled and peeled
2 tablespoons green onion, diced
2 tablespoons fresh cilantro, minced
2 small mild chile peppers, minced
½ cup mayonnaise
2 teaspoons prepared mustard
1 teaspoon salt
Black pepper, to taste
½ cup cheese, shredded
Chili powder, for garnish

Slice hardboiled eggs lengthwise. Scoop out yolks and place in a medium bowl. Add green onions, cilantro, chile peppers, mayonnaise, mustard, salt, pepper, and cheese to the yolks; mix until well combined. Fill egg whites with the yolk mixture. Sprinkle with chili powder and chill before serving.

—*Tamara*, KENTUCKY

Horseradish Deviled Eggs

Makes 12 Deviled Eggs

6 eggs, hard-boiled, shells removed
¼ cup mayonnaise
1 to 2 tablespoons prepared horseradish
½ teaspoon dill weed
¼ teaspoon ground mustard
$1/8$ teaspoon salt
Dash of pepper
Paprika, for garnish

Cut hard-boiled eggs in half lengthwise. Remove yolks and place in bowl; set whites aside. Mash the yolks. Add mayonnaise, horseradish, dill, mustard, salt, and pepper. Mix well. Spoon yolk mixture onto egg whites. Sprinkle with paprika. Refrigerate until serving time.

—*Mildred*, LOUISIANA

*Of course,
the finest way to know
that the egg you plan to eat
is a fresh one is to own
the hen that makes the egg.*

—M. F. K. FISHER

Cheese Straws

Makes 24 Straws

½ pound extra sharp Cheddar cheese, shredded
1 stick (½ cup) butter; softened, not melted
1½ cups flour, sifted
½ teaspoon baking powder
½ teaspoon salt
Hot pepper, to taste

Preheat oven to 350°F. Mix the grated cheese with the butter in a large bowl. In a separate bowl, combine flour, baking powder, and salt; sift. Gradually mix the dry ingredients with the cheese mixture. Add hot pepper to taste. Mix well. Work into a ball and then roll out flat with a rolling pin until ½-inch thick. Use a cookie cutter or knife to cut into desired shape. Place on cookie sheet and bake for about 8 minutes. Watch baking progress closely and remove from cookie sheet promptly to prevent burning. Place on a wire rack to cool.

—Eunice, MISSISSIPPI

Barbecued Meatballs

These meatballs can be made ahead and frozen.

Makes 36 Small Meatballs

MEATBALLS:
1½ pounds ground beef
1 (5-ounce) can evaporated milk
1 egg, beaten
1 cup quick oats
½ cup onion, chopped
1 teaspoon salt
1 teaspoon chili powder
¼ teaspoon garlic powder
¼ teaspoon pepper

SAUCE:
1 cup ketchup
¼ cup onion, chopped
¾ cup brown sugar
1 teaspoon liquid smoke
¼ teaspoon garlic powder

Meatballs: Preheat oven to 350°F. In a large bowl, combine all meatball ingredients and shape into walnut-size balls. Place in a 9x13-inch baking pan.

Sauce: In a saucepan, combine all sauce ingredients. Cook over medium heat and stir until sugar dissolves.

Pour sauce over meatballs. Cover and bake for 45–50 minutes. Uncover and bake an additional 5–10 minutes to brown.

—*Jeanette*, VIRGINIA

Fried Dill Pickles

Makes 24 Fried Dill Pickles

Vegetable oil, for frying
1 (24-ounce) jar kosher dill pickles, sliced;
  2 tablespoons juice reserved
1 cup flour
1 teaspoon garlic powder
1 teaspoon ground red pepper
¼ teaspoon salt
1 cup club soda, chilled

In a Dutch oven, add oil until 3 inches in depth. Heat oil to 370°F. Drain pickles, reserving 2 tablespoons pickle juice. Dry pickles by pressing between layers of paper towels; set dry pickles aside. In a medium bowl, combine flour, garlic powder, red pepper, and salt. Stir in chilled club soda and reserved 2 tablespoons pickle juice until just combined. Batter will be lumpy. Dip pickles into batter and allow excess batter to drip back into bowl before frying. Place pickles in heated oil in Dutch oven. Fry pickles in small batches, about 2½ minutes for each batch, or until golden brown. Drain on wire racks placed over paper towels. Serve warm.

—*Ceil*, ARKANSAS

In the last analysis,
a pickle
is nothing more than
a cucumber
with experience.

—IRENA CHALMERS

Shrimp in Dijon Vinaigrette

Makes 12 Servings

3 pounds large shrimp
2 teaspoons salt, for boiling
½ cup fresh parsley, finely chopped
½ cup shallots, finely chopped
½ cup tarragon vinegar
1 cup olive oil
8 tablespoons Dijon mustard
4 teaspoons red pepper flakes
1 teaspoon fresh lemon juice
Freshly ground black pepper, to taste

In a large pot, add water and salt. Bring salted water to a boil and cook the shrimp until pink. Drain, peel shrimp, and place in a large bowl. Combine remaining 8 ingredients and pour over warm shrimp. Toss well. Cover and refrigerate at least 8 hours. Drain excess liquid before serving.

—*Meg*, ALABAMA

Black Bean Spirals

For a Crowd

Makes 30 Appetizers

8 ounces cream cheese
1 cup Monterey Jack cheese, shredded
1 (4-ounce) can diced chilies
½ cup sour cream
½ cup green onions, chopped
1 (15-ounce) can black beans, drained and rinsed
4 (10-inch) flour tortillas

Using an electric mixer, beat cheeses, chilies, sour cream, onions, and beans until well blended. Spread ¼ of the mixture onto each of the tortillas. Roll tortillas tightly and refrigerate at least 30 minutes. Cut into 1-inch slices and serve.

—*Krista*, NORTH CAROLINA

Sausage Won Ton Stars

For a Crowd

Makes 48 Appetizers

1 (12-ounce) package won ton wrappers
1 pound ground pork sausage
2 cups colby cheese, shredded
½ green bell pepper, chopped
½ red bell pepper, chopped
2 bunches green onions, sliced
½ cup ranch dressing

Preheat oven to 350°F. In a greased miniature muffin pan, lightly press a won ton wrapper into the bottom and up the sides of each cup. Bake until edges are browned, about 5 minutes. In a large skillet, cook sausage until no longer pink; drain. Stir in cheese, peppers, onions, and salad dressing. Spoon a rounded tablespoon of sausage mixture into each wonton cup. Bake until heated through, about 6–7 minutes.

—*Norma*, ARKANSAS

Stuffed Mushrooms

Makes 36 Stuffed Mushrooms

36 fresh mushrooms, reserve 12–18 stems
1 (8-ounce) package cream cheese
6 ounces crabmeat
½ teaspoon garlic salt
Bunch of green onions, chopped (optional)
4 strips of bacon, cooked and crumbled (optional)

Preheat oven to 350°F. Lightly grease a baking sheet with non-stick cooking spray. Stem the mushrooms. Reserve and mince 12–18 of the stems. In a bowl, whip the cream cheese until smooth and set aside. In a small bowl, combine minced mushroom stems and crabmeat. Blend the cream cheese into the stem and crab mixture. Add garlic salt and mix well. Stuff mushrooms. Arrange the caps on the prepared baking sheet. Bake for 20 minutes. Place caps under the broiler and broil for an additional 2 minutes. Add a bunch of chopped green onions and cooked, crumbled bacon for a bit of zip. If adding the extras, it will be best to use only 12 of the reserved stems or you will have too much stuffing.

—*Susan,* ARKANSAS

Italian Artichoke Crostini

For a Crowd

Makes 20 Appetizers

1 (14-ounce) can artichoke hearts in water,
    drained and chopped
½ cup red bell pepper, finely diced
1¼ cups mozzarella cheese, shredded, divided
1 teaspoon lemon zest
¼ cup mayonnaise
1 garlic clove, pressed
1½ teaspoons Italian seasoning, divided
20 (¼-inch thick) slices French bread, lightly toasted
2 Roma tomatoes, sliced
1 small zucchini, sliced

Preheat oven to 400°F. In a large bowl, combine artichoke hearts, bell pepper, 1 cup of cheese, lemon zest, mayonnaise, garlic, and 1 teaspoon of the Italian seasoning; mix well. Arrange bread slices on baking sheets. Divide filling evenly between bread slices. Top each crostini with a tomato or a zucchini slice.

In a small bowl, combine ¼ cup of cheese with ½ teaspoon Italian seasoning; sprinkle over tomato and zucchini slices. Bake until light golden brown, 15–18 minutes. Serve hot.

—*Jessica and Tanya,* TENNESSEE

Crab Bites

These can be made ahead and frozen.
Makes 48 Crab Bites

6 ounces fresh or canned lump crabmeat, drained
1 (5-ounce) jar Kraft Old English Sharp Cheddar Cheese™
1 tablespoon mayonnaise
Garlic salt, to taste
6 English muffins, sliced in half
Paprika, for garnish

Preheat oven to 350°F. Mix crabmeat, cheese, mayonnaise, and garlic salt. Spread mixture generously on English muffin halves. Cut muffins into quarters. Transfer to cookie sheet. Bake for 15–20 minutes. Sprinkle with paprika and serve hot.

—*Dianne,* MISSISSIPPI

Okra Roll-Ups

Makes 16 Roll-Ups

1 (8-ounce) package cream cheese, softened
½ teaspoon lemon pepper
½ teaspoon garlic powder
1 pound ham, thinly sliced
2 (12-ounce) jars pickled okra

In a large bowl, mix cream cheese, lemon pepper, and garlic powder. Place ham slices on a large cookie sheet. Spread the cream cheese mixture on the ham slices. Cut ends off of the okra. Place 1 or 2 pieces of okra lengthwise on ham slices and roll ham around okra. Chill for several hours. Cut each roll in half.

—*Diane,* LOUISIANA

Delicious Baked Oysters

Makes 8 to 10 Servings

1 stick (½ cup) butter
½ cup olive oil
½ cup green onions, chopped
2 cloves garlic, finely chopped
1⅓ cups breadcrumbs
½ cup Parmesan cheese, grated
1 teaspoon salt
½ teaspoon pepper
¼ teaspoon cayenne pepper
1 teaspoon basil
1 teaspoon oregano
12 oysters, shelled

Preheat oven to 425°F. In large skillet over medium heat, combine butter and olive oil. When butter has melted, add onions and garlic. Sauté for 5 minutes. In a small bowl, combine breadcrumbs, cheese, salt, peppers, basil, and oregano. Add combined ingredients in bowl to mixture in skillet and stir. Remove from heat and add the oysters. Stir well. Transfer to baking dish and bake for 15 minutes until crusty and brown.

—*Jane*, MISSISSIPPI

Mississippi Sour Bread

Makes 18 Servings

1 loaf sourdough bread
1 (8-ounce) package cream cheese, softened
1 (16-ounce) carton sour cream
2 cups Cheddar cheese, shredded
1 cup ham, cooked and chopped
1 (4-ounce) can green chiles, chopped
2 teaspoons Worcestershire sauce
Frito Scoops™ or Wheat Thins,™ for serving

Preheat oven to 350°F. Slice and remove the top third of bread loaf. Scoop out center of loaf leaving a ¾-inch wall of bread to make a bowl. Mix 6 filling ingredients and spoon into the bread bowl. Wrap bread bowl in aluminum foil and bake for 1 hour. Serve with Frito Scoops™ or Wheat Thins.™

—*Patsy,* ALABAMA

Spicy Red Pecans

Makes 12 Servings

¼ cup butter or margarine
1–2 teaspoons ground red chile pepper, to taste
¾ to 1 teaspoon garlic salt
3 cups pecan halves

In a large skillet, melt butter over medium heat. Add chile pepper, garlic salt, and pecans. Stir for 4–5 minutes until pecans are browned and well coated.

—*Wyonnie*, GEORGIA

Spiced Pecans

Makes 8 to 10 Servings

½ cup water
1¼ cups sugar
1½ teaspoons cinnamon
¼ teaspoon salt
1 teaspoon vanilla
1 pound pecans, toasted

In a saucepan, mix water, sugar, cinnamon, and salt. Cook over medium-low heat until mixture is gummy. Add vanilla and toasted pecans. Stir until pecans are well coated.

—*Jennifer*, NORTH CAROLINA

White Chocolate Party Mix

For a Crowd

Party mix can be frozen for up to a month.

Makes 16 Cups

1 (14-ounce) package chocolate covered peanuts
1 (9-ounce) package pretzels
5 cups Cheerios™
5 cups corn flakes
1½ pounds white chocolate

Combine chocolate covered peanuts. pretzels, Cherrios,™ and corn flakes in a large, tempered glass bowl; set aside. In a microwave-safe bowl, microwave white chocolate on high for 1 minute, stirring once. Microwave for one additional minute, stirring every 15 seconds, until chocolate is smooth and melted. Immediately pour white chocolate over cereal mix; stir to combine. Spread mixture onto wax paper and let cool for 30 minutes. Break apart and store in an airtight container.

—*Linda,* NORTH CAROLINA

Salads, Soups, Stews, and Sandwiches

For those who love it,
cooking is at once child's play
and adult joy.
And cooking done with care
is an act of love.

—CRAIG CLAIBORNE

Peach Salad with Raspberry Dressing

Makes 4 to 5 Servings

SALAD:

1 (3-ounce) package lemon Jell-O™

1 cup boiling water

½ teaspoon celery salt

⅛ teaspoon paprika

½ teaspoon dry mustard

1 teaspoon cider vinegar

2 cups fresh peaches, diced

1 cup homemade heavy whipping cream

Salad greens, for serving

DRESSING:

½ cup raspberries, puréed

2 tablespoons mayonnaise

¼ cup sour cream

Sugar, to taste

Salad: Oil a 4–5 cup mold. Pour Jell-O™ package contents into a large mixing bowl. Add boiling water and stir until dissolved. Add celery, salt, paprika, and dry mustard; stir until smooth. Add vinegar and peaches. Blend well. Gently fold in whipping cream and pour into mold. Refrigerate until firm.

Dressing: Combine all ingredients and stir until well blended. Chill thoroughly.

At serving time, remove from mold and place on salad greens. Serve with raspberry dressing.

—*Dorothy*, LOUISIANA

Good For You Salad

Makes 6 Servings

1 head romaine lettuce, chopped
1 bunch fresh spinach, chopped
½ red onion, thinly sliced
2 tablespoons goat cheese, crumbled
3 tablespoons pecans, toasted and chopped
2 cups chicken, cooked and chopped (optional)
Raspberry vinaigrette, for serving

In a large salad bowl, toss all ingredients except the dressing.
Serve raspberry vinaigrette on the side.

—*Pam,* KENTUCKY

Ambrosia

Makes 6 to 8 Servings

1 (20-ounce) can pineapple chunks, drained
1 (11-ounce) can Mandarin oranges, drained
1½ cups seedless grapes
1 cup miniature marshmallows
1 cup flaked coconut
½ cup pecans, chopped
8 ounces sour cream
1 tablespoon sugar

In a large bowl, combine pineapple, oranges, grapes, marshmallows,
coconut, and pecans. In a small bowl, mix sour cream and sugar.
Add mixture in small bowl to the ingredients in the large bowl
and stir to combine. Chill at least 3 hours or overnight, if possible.

—*Judy,* NORTH CAROLINA

Wilted Lettuce Salad

Makes 6 Servings

6 strips bacon; cooked and crumbled, grease reserved
¼ cup vinegar
¼ cup brown sugar
Salt, to taste
Pepper, to taste
1 large head green leaf lettuce, leaves coarsely torn
4 radishes, thinly sliced
½ medium onion, chopped

Fry bacon in a skillet. Remove bacon from pan; reserve grease. Crumble bacon when cool. In a small bowl, mix vinegar and brown sugar; add salt and pepper to taste. Pour vinegar/brown sugar mixture into skillet with bacon grease and warm over medium heat.

In a salad bowl, combine lettuce, radishes, and onion. When dressing is desired temperature, pour it over the salad. Top with crumbled bacon and serve immediately.

—Jo, ARKANSAS

Georgia Cracker Salad

Makes 6 Servings

1 sleeve (about 36) saltine crackers
1 large tomato, chopped
1 hard-boiled egg, diced
3 green onions, chopped
1½ cups mayonnaise
Salt and pepper, for seasoning

Break the crackers into large pieces and place into a medium bowl. Add the remaining ingredients and mix well. Season to taste with salt and pepper. Serve immediately.

—Cathy, GEORGIA

Whole Earth Salad

Makes 10 Servings

BAKED TOFU:
2 (12-ounce) blocks tofu, rinsed and drained
½ cup soy sauce   4 cloves garlic, minced
Pepper, to taste

SALAD:
2 bunches raw kale, washed and well drained
2 carrots, peeled and shredded
2 cups brown rice, cooked and cooled
½ cup almonds, chopped
½ cup sunflower seeds, toasted
¼ cup sesame seeds, toasted

DRESSING:
2 large lemons, juiced   1 cup olive oil
6 cloves garlic, minced   2 teaspoons dry mustard
2 teaspoons sea salt   2 teaspoons honey

Tofu: Cut tofu crosswise into ½-inch slices. Place flat on paper towels and cover with more paper towels. Place a cutting board on top of tofu and allow weighted tofu to rest for at least ½ hour to express water. Cut slices into ½-inch cubes. Place in a glass container or zip lock bag with soy sauce, garlic, and pepper. Allow tofu to marinate for several hours.

Preheat oven to 350°F. Arrange marinated tofu cubes on a cookie sheet lined with lightly greased aluminum foil. Bake until brown and bubbling, about 30 minutes. Allow to cool.

Salad: Cut stem and central rib from kale, splitting leaf in half. Stack several leaves together, roll them up like a cigar, and cut into narrow strips with kitchen scissors. Place the kale in a large bowl, add shredded carrots, and chill.

Dressing: Mix all dressing ingredients in a blender.

When ready to serve, add cooked and cooled rice, tofu, almonds, toasted sesame and sunflower seeds; toss gently. Add dressing and toss again.

—*Sue*, LOUISIANA

Classic Slaw

Makes 6 to 8 Servings

2 cups cabbage, shredded
1 cup apples, diced
½ cup walnuts, chopped
¼ cup raisins
½ cup carrots, grated
1 tablespoon sugar
½ teaspoon lemon juice
½ cup whipping cream
¼ cup mayonnaise

Combine cabbage, apples, walnuts, raisins, and carrots in a large bowl. Set aside. In a small bowl, whisk sugar, lemon juice, whipping cream, and mayonnaise. Fold liquid ingredients into the cabbage mixture and toss to combine. Refrigerate. Serve chilled.

—*Karen,* SOUTH CAROLINA

Shrimp Salad

Makes 4 to 6 Servings

1 pound shrimp
Zatarain's™ Crab Boil, to taste
3 eggs, hard-boiled, shells removed, eggs chopped
4 green onions, chopped
1 tablespoon lemon juice
3 tablespoons sweet pickle relish
½ cup mayonnaise

In a large pot over high heat, add Crab Boil to water and bring to a boil. Add shrimp and cook until pink, about 3 minutes. Drain and peel. Chop shrimp. Place shrimp in a large bowl and combine with remaining ingredients; stir. Cover and refrigerate.

—*Bobbie,* MISSISSIPPI

Okra Salad

Makes 6 Servings

Shortening, for frying
1 cup flour
1 cup cornmeal
1 pound okra, washed and cut lengthwise into thin strips
½ onion, diced
2 medium tomatoes, diced
Salt and pepper, to taste

Melt the shortening in a large skillet. In a wide, shallow container, combine the flour and cornmeal. Roll okra in the mixture. Add coated okra to skillet and fry until okra is dark golden brown. Place cooked okra in a bowl and cover with diced onions. Top with tomatoes; add salt and pepper to taste.

—*Wilma*, KENTUCKY

Health conscious gumbo lovers rejoice! Okra is not just an extremely practical ingredient used to thicken your gumbo. This softly textured, delicately flavored vegetable provides a good supply of fiber to your diet. An ample amount of protein, calcium, vitamins A and B, and potassium add nutritional value.

Shoepeg Salad

Makes 6 to 8 Servings

SALAD:
1 (16-ounce) can LaSeur Baby Peas,™ drained
1 (16-ounce) can shoepeg corn, drained
1 green pepper, chopped
1 small bunch green onions, chopped
1 (2-ounce) jar pimentos

DRESSING:
³/₈ cup vinegar
½ tablespoon water
¼ cup oil
½ teaspoon salt
½ teaspoon pepper
½ cup sugar

Salad: In a large bowl, combine all salad ingredients; stir and set aside.

Dressing: In a small saucepan, combine all dressing ingredients; mix and bring to a boil. Remove from heat and cool.

Add dressing to the salad, cover, and refrigerate overnight.

—*Cynthia*, VIRGINIA

Barbequed Bean Salad

Makes 10 Servings

1 pound dry pinto beans
¼ cup cider vinegar
¼ cup vegetable oil
¼ cup ketchup
¼ cup brown sugar, packed
1 tablespoon Dijon mustard
1 tablespoon Worcestershire sauce
2 teaspoons chili powder
¾ teaspoon ground cumin
1 teaspoon salt
¼ teaspoon pepper
¼ teaspoon hot pepper sauce
1 (15¼-ounce) can corn, drained
1 medium red bell pepper, chopped
1 medium onion, chopped
2 cups tortilla chips, coarsely crushed, divided

Place beans in a Dutch oven; add enough water to measure 2 inches above the beans. Bring water to a boil and boil for 2 minutes. Remove from heat; cover and let stand for 1 hour. Drain and discard liquid. Add enough water to measure 2 inches above the beans. Bring to a boil. Reduce heat; cover and simmer for 1–1½ hours or until beans are tender. Rinse beans, drain, and set aside.

In a saucepan, combine vinegar, oil, ketchup, brown sugar, mustard, Worcestershire sauce, chili powder, cumin, salt, pepper, and hot pepper sauce. Bring to a boil. Reduce heat; cover, and simmer for 10 minutes. Remove from heat and set aside to cool slightly.

In a large salad bowl, combine cooked beans, corn, peppers, and onion; toss to combine. Just before serving, stir dressing and half of the chips into the salad. Sprinkle with the remaining chips and serve.

—*Barbara*, SOUTH CAROLINA

Black-Eyed Pea Salad

Makes 10 to 12 Servings

2 (15-ounce) cans Trappey's™ Jalapeño Black Eye Peas
   Flavored with Slab Bacon, drained
1 green bell pepper, chopped
1–2 avocados, chopped
½ green onion including top, chopped
1 pint (16-ounces) cherry tomatoes, sliced
1 (4-ounce) jar pimentos
¼ cup celery, sliced
1 (8-ounce) bottle Catalina dressing
Minced garlic, to taste
Salt and pepper, to taste
Fritos Scoops,™ for serving

In a large bowl, mix all ingredients except the Fritos.™ Cover and refrigerate overnight to allow flavors to blend. Serve with Fritos Scoops.™

—*Betty*, ARKANSAS

Yam Raisin Salad

Makes 10 to 12 Servings

3 cups yams, shredded and lightly steamed
½ cup flaked coconut
½ cup raisins
⅓ cup mayonnaise
¼ cup pineapple juice
⅓ cup walnuts or pecans, chopped (optional)
Lettuce leaves, for serving

In a large bowl, combine all ingredients except the lettuce. Mix well. Cover and refrigerate for 2 hours. Serve on lettuce leaves.

—*Linda*, LOUISIANA

Warm Mustard Potato Salad

Makes 6 Servings

2 pounds small red potatoes
1 cup mayonnaise
¼ cup Dijon mustard
½ cup red onion, chopped
2 whole green onions, sliced
2 garlic cloves, minced
3 tablespoons fresh dill, minced
½ teaspoon salt
½ teaspoon pepper
¼ teaspoon fresh lime juice

Place potatoes in a large pot. Fill pot with enough water to cover potatoes. Cover the pot and bring water to a boil. Reduce heat and simmer until potatoes are tender, about 25 minutes. Drain water and allow potatoes to cool slightly. In a large bowl, combine the remaining ingredients. Remove potatoes from the pot and cut into chunks. Add potatoes to the dressing; toss to coat. Serve warm.

—*Barbara*, SOUTH CAROLINA

There is no species of human food that can be consumed in a greater variety of modes than the potato.

—SIR JOHN SINCLAIR

Picnic Potato Salad

Makes 10 to 12 Servings

3 pounds small red potatoes, cut into 1-inch cubes
2½ teaspoons salt, divided
1 cup refrigerated French onion dip
1 tablespoon brown sugar, firmly packed
¼ teaspoon black pepper, coarsely ground
1 cup celery, sliced
½ cup red onion, sliced
3 eggs, hard-boiled, shells removed, eggs chopped
Sliced hard-boiled egg, for garnish, if desired

Place cubed potatoes in a 4-quart pot. Cover with water and add 1 teaspoon salt; cover and bring to a boil over medium-high heat. Cook 8–10 minutes or until tender. Transfer potatoes to colander and drain. Cool to room temperature. In a large bowl, combine onion dip, sugar, pepper, and remaining 1½ teaspoons salt. Add potatoes, celery, onion, and eggs. Mix gently. Cover and refrigerate at least 2 hours or overnight. Garnish the salad with a sliced hard-boiled egg, if desired.

—*T.R.*, ARKANSAS

" *It's a lovely thing—
everyone sitting down together,
sharing food.* "

—ALICE MAY BROCK

Curry Rice Salad

This salad can be served hot or cold.
Makes 10 to 12 Servings

SALAD:

1 (7-ounce) package Zatarain's™ Long Grain
    and Wild Rice Mix
2 cups chicken broth
1 cup raisins
1 cup very hot water
½ cup green onions, chopped
1 cup pecans, toasted and chopped
1 (16-ounce) can garbanzo beans, drained

DRESSING:

$^2/_3$ cup mayonnaise
1 tablespoon honey
$^1/_8$ teaspoon ground red pepper
1 teaspoon Worcestershire sauce
1 tablespoon curry powder
1 tablespoon vinegar
2 teaspoons prepared mustard

Salad: In a saucepan, combine rice mix and broth. Bring to a boil over medium-high heat. Reduce heat and cover. Simmer until liquid is absorbed, 20–25 minutes. Place raisins in a cup of very hot water and let stand for 10 minutes. Drain. Stir raisins, chopped onions, toasted and chopped pecans, and garbanzo beans into the cooked rice.

Dressing: In a medium bowl, combine all dressing ingredients and mix well.

Add dressing to the salad and stir.

—*Kella*, LOUISIANA

Cornbread Salad

Makes 16 to 18 Servings

1 package Jiffy™ Corn Muffin Mix
3 large tomatoes, chopped
½ cup green onions, chopped
½ cup green peppers, chopped
1 cup mayonnaise
1 cup sour cream
1 (1-ounce) package ranch-style dressing mix
2 (15-ounce) cans pinto beans, drained
2 (15-ounce) cans whole kernel corn, drained
½ cup red peppers, chopped
10 slices bacon, cooked crisp and crumbled
2 cups Cheddar cheese, shredded

Prepare cornbread according to package directions. Cool, crumble, and set aside. In a medium bowl, mix the chopped tomatoes, green onions, and peppers. In a separate bowl, mix the mayonnaise, sour cream, and ranch dressing. In a large, wide-bottomed, shallow dish, layer half of the crumbled cornbread, followed by half of the tomato mixture, half of the beans, half of the corn, half of the bacon, and half of the mayonnaise mixture. Finish with half of the cheese. Repeat layers with the remaining ingredients.

—*Daisy*, ALABAMA

Macaroni Salad

For a Crowd

Makes 100 Servings

SALAD:

5–6 pounds chicken or ham, cooked and cubed

5–6 pounds macaroni, cooked and drained

3 pounds Cheddar cheese, shredded

2 (20-ounce) bags frozen peas, thawed

2 bunches celery, chopped

2 large onions, chopped

2 (5 ¾-ounce) cans sliced black olives

DRESSING:

2 quarts mayonnaise

1 (8-ounce) bottle French salad dressing

¼ cup vinegar

¼ cup sugar

1 cup light cream

1½ teaspoons onion salt

1½ teaspoons garlic salt

1 teaspoon salt

1 teaspoon pepper

Salad: In a very large bowl, combine all salad ingredients; toss to mix.

Dressing: In a separate large bowl, combine all dressing ingredients and stir to mix well.

Pour dressing over the macaroni mixture, tossing lightly. Refrigerate. Serve chilled.

—*Jan,* ALABAMA

Cold Strawberry Soup

Makes 8 Servings

VANILLA SUGAR:

1 vanilla bean

2 cups sugar

SOUP:

¾ pound ripe strawberries,
   washed, hulled, and halved

2 tablespoons vanilla sugar

¼ cup sugar

¾ pound ripe strawberries,
   washed, hulled, and left whole

4 cups fruit stock

Zest of 1 small lemon

2 tablespoons cornstarch

Sour cream, for garnish

Sliced bananas, for garnish

Vanilla sugar: Place sugar in an airtight container. Slice down the back of the vanilla bean and scrape the seed into jar with sugar. Bury vanilla in the sugar. Seal container tightly and let sit for at least a week before using. Use the leftover sugar in coffee, smoothies, mixed drinks, over cereal, or anywhere you would use regular sugar.

Soup: Place halved berries in a medium bowl and sprinkle with sugars. Set aside and let stand for at least 20 minutes. In a saucepan, add the whole berries and fruit stock; bring to a boil. Allow berries and stock to boil for 10 minutes. Add lemon juice and zest. In a small bowl, whisk a little of the stock into the cornstarch until it is smooth. Whisk the moistened cornstarch into the soup. Cook for an additional 10 minutes. Allow soup to cool before refrigerating. Serve cold, garnished with halved starwberries, sour cream, and sliced bananas.

—*Linda*, LOUISIANA

Cream of Pecan Soup

Makes 8 Servings

1 stick (½ cup) butter
½ cup onions, chopped
2 tablespoons flour
4 cups milk
1 (15-ounce) can cream of potato soup
2 cups pecan meal
1 clove garlic, crushed
2 tablespoons parsley, chopped
2 tablespoons green onions, chopped
½–¾ tablespoon salt
Tabasco™ sauce, to taste
Pinch of nutmeg
1 cup heavy cream

In a large pot, sauté onions in butter until limp. Add flour and stir constantly until smooth. Add milk and stir until mixture comes to a boil. Reduce heat and add remaining ingredients, stirring often. Simmer for 5 minutes. Serve at once.

—*Oma*, LOUISIANA

If someone in the vicinity of New Orleans mentions that you have "gone pecan," these words are probably meant in a most good-natured way. This phrase is used to describe a person who is behaving a bit beyond the realm of reason. By the way, the regional pronunciation is "gawn pe-cawn."

Turnip Green Soup

Makes 10 Servings

1 pound country ham, cubed
2 cups chicken broth
2 medium red potatoes, chopped
¼ cup onions
½ cup carrots, sliced
½ cup celery, chopped
2 (15-ounce) cans navy beans
2 (10-ounce) packages frozen turnip greens
1 tablespoon sugar
Salt and pepper, to taste
Garlic powder, to taste

In a large pot, add ham, chicken broth, potatoes, onions, carrots, and celery. Bring to a boil over high heat; reduce heat, cover, and simmer for 10 minutes. Stir in navy beans, turnip greens, and sugar. Season with salt, pepper, and garlic powder. Return to a boil. Reduce heat and simmer for 1 hour.

—*Toodlum,* MISSISSIPPI

Black-Eyed Pea and Mustard Greens Soup

Makes 10 to 12 Servings

PEAS:
1 pound (2 cups) dried black-eyed peas
2½ quarts chicken stock

SOUP:
¼ cup butter or margarine

2 cups onions, diced

1 cup celery, diced

½ cup red bell pepper, diced

¼ cup garlic, diced

1 pound smoked sausage, diced

1 bay leaf

1 sprig fresh thyme or a dash of dried thyme

10 ounces cut mustard greens

½ cup tomatoes, peeled and diced

¼ cup green onions, sliced

¼ cup parsley

Salt, to taste

Pepper, to taste

Tobasco™ sauce, to taste

Peas: Wash dried black-eyed peas and soak them in water for at least 1 hour and up to 24 hours. Drain. Combine peas and chicken stock in a medium pot over medium-low heat. Cover and simmer 1 hour or until tender. Add water if needed to keep peas submerged. When tender, mash about one half of the peas.

Soup: Melt butter in a large pot. Sauté onions, celery, bell pepper, and garlic until vegetables are tender, about 5–7 minutes. Add the sausage, bay leaf, and thyme to the vegetable mixture and sauté 5 minutes more. Stir in the black-eyed peas, and then add the mustard greens, tomatoes, green onions, and parsley. Season with salt, pepper, and Tobasco™ sauce. Simmer for 30 minutes. Serve hot. This recipe sounds difficult but it really is easy. It just takes a little time to prepare.

—*Faye,* MISSISSIPPI

Sauerkraut Soup

Makes 8 to 10 Servings

1 (16-ounce) jar sauerkraut
1 (15-ounce) can black-eyed peas
1 pound smoked sausage, chopped
5 medium potatoes, cubed
1 large onion, cubed
1 (15-ounce) can tomato sauce
2 tablespoons sugar
½ teaspoon salt
½ teaspoon black pepper
¼ teaspoon cayenne pepper
¼ teaspoon caraway seeds

In a large soup pot, combine sauerkraut, black-eyed peas, sausage, potatoes, onion, tomato sauce, sugar, salt, peppers, and caraway seeds. Cover with enough water to reach 2 inches above the ingredients. Cook for 45 minutes.

—*Jo Ann,* MISSISSIPPI

Onion Soup

Makes 8 Servings

4 onions, very thinly sliced
½ cup butter
2 tablespoons flour
4 cups chicken stock, heated
Salt, to taste
Pepper, to taste
8 slices French bread
½ cup Parmesan cheese

Melt the butter in a large saucepan. Add onions and cook until tender, but not browned. Add flour and blend well. Slowly add the hot chicken stock, stirring constantly. Season with salt and pepper. Toast the bread, sprinkle with Parmesan cheese, and broil until the cheese is slightly melted. Spoon soup into 8 bowls and top each one with a slice of the bread. Serve immediately.

—*Linda,* MISSISSIPPI

" *Life is like an onion.*
You peel it off one layer at a time;
and sometimes you weep. "

—CARL SANDBURG

Spicy Winter Squash Soup

Makes 6 Servings

2 tablespoons extra virgin olive oil

1 large Vidalia onion, chopped

3 celery stalks, chopped

4 cloves garlic, minced

1 tablespoon Madras-style curry powder

1½ pounds butternut squash, pared

2 green plantains, peeled and cubed

6 cups chicken broth

2 sprigs fresh oregano or ½ teaspoon dried oregano

2 sprigs fresh sage or ½ teaspoon dried sage

½ teaspoon hot red pepper sauce

Salt, to taste

Freshly ground black pepper, to taste

¼ cup pumpkin seeds, toasted, for garnish

Fresh chives, chopped, for garnish

In a large pot, heat the oil over medium-low heat. Add the onion and celery; cover. Cook, stirring occasionally, until the onion is translucent, about 8 minutes. Add the garlic and cook for 1 minute. Add the curry powder and cook, stirring until fragrant, about 30 seconds. Stir in the squash and plantains, then the broth, oregano, and sage. Bring to a boil over high heat. Reduce the heat to low and simmer, partially covered, until the squash is very tender, about 20 minutes. Remove from heat. In batches, pulse the soup in a blender or food processor to make a chunky purée. Return to the pot and season to taste with the hot sauce, salt, and pepper. Reheat until piping hot. Pour in soup bowls and garnish with pumpkin seeds and chives.

—*Hazel*, MISSISSIPPI

Spicy Potato Soup

Makes 6 to 8 Servings

1 pound ground beef
4 cups potatoes, peeled and cubed
1 small onion, chopped
3 (8-ounce) cans tomato sauce
4 cups water
2 teaspoons salt
1½ teaspoons black pepper
½–1 tablespoon hot pepper sauce

In a large pot over medium-high heat, brown ground beef; drain.
Add cubed potatoes, chopped onion, and tomato sauce to the
ground beef. Stir in water, salt, pepper, and hot pepper sauce;
bring to a boil. Reduce heat and simmer until the potatoes are
tender and the soup has thickened, about 1 hour.

—*Lois,* KENTUCKY

So you have a kinder, more adaptable friend

in the food world than soup?

Who soothes you when you are ill?

…Who warms you in the winter and

cools you in the summer? …Soup does its loyal best….

You don't catch steak hanging around

when you're poor and sick, do you?

—JUDITH MARTIN (MISS MANNERS)

Leek & Potato Soup
with Spinach & Turnips

For a Crowd

Sprinkle this soup with fresh chives and serve it for lunch,
or turn it into a hearty meal by topping it off with chopped lobster,
Dungeness crab, shrimp, or finely chopped ham. Serve hot or chilled.
This soup can be frozen for later use.

Makes 15 to 20 Servings

3–4 large leeks, rootlets trimmed and green stems discarded

1 large onion, finely chopped

4 tablespoons butter

2 quarts (8 cups) chicken stock

6 medium potatoes, peeled and cubed, or sliced in food processor

3–4 small turnips, cubed

1 (12-ounce) bag fresh baby spinach

1 quart (4 cups) cream or milk

Salt, to taste

Freshly ground black pepper, to taste

Slit leeks lengthwise and rinse well under cold water. Leeks are very sandy and must be washed thoroughly. Dice the leeks. Set aside. In a medium skillet, sauté leeks with onions and butter for 3–5 minutes. In a large pot, add chicken stock and bring to a boil. Add potatoes, turnips, sautéed onion, and leek mixture to the large pot and return to a boil. Reduce heat, add spinach and simmer for about 15 minutes or until ingredients are tender. Pour soup into a blender until $2/3$ full. Hold top down firmly when starting the blender and purée. Pour puréed mixture into a separate large container until entire soup mixture is processed. Return puréed mixture to the soup pot. Add cream, and season with salt and freshly ground pepper. Bring to gentle simmer over low heat, stirring occasionally. Do not boil!

If you want to make basic potato leek soup, you can omit the spinach and turnips and add extra potatoes, or decrease the amounts on the liquid ingredients.

—*Frances*, SOUTH CAROLINA

Roasted Chicken Noodle Soup

Makes 10 to 12 Servings

2 teaspoons olive oil
1 cup onion, chopped
1 cup carrots, diced
1 cup celery, sliced
1 clove garlic, minced
¼ cup flour
½ teaspoon dried oregano
¼ teaspoon dried thyme
¼ teaspoon poultry seasoning
6 cups low salt chicken broth
4 cups baking potatoes, peeled and diced
1 teaspoon salt
2 cups leftover roasted chicken, diced
1 cup evaporated skim milk
4 ounces (2 cups) uncooked wide egg noodles

In a Dutch oven, heat olive oil over medium heat. Add chopped onion, carrots, celery, and garlic; sauté for 5 minutes. Sprinkle flour, oregano, thyme, and poultry seasoning over vegetables and cook for 1 minute. Stir in broth, potatoes, and salt. Bring to a boil. Reduce heat, and simmer partially uncovered until potatoes are tender, about 25 minutes. Add roasted chicken, milk, and noodles. Cook until noodles are tender, about 10 minutes.

—*Vicky*, VIRGINIA

Worries go down better with soup.

–YIDDISH PROVERB

Pig's Feet Soup

Makes 6 to 8 Servings

1 tablespoon vinegar
1½ pounds pig's feet
2 teaspoons salt
Pepper, to taste
2 tomatoes, chopped
1 cup lima beans, cooked
1 cup corn, cooked

In a large stockpot, add vinegar, pig's feet, salt, pepper, and enough water to cover pig's feet. Cover and bring to a boil. Reduce heat to medium-low and simmer until meat is tender. Stir in tomatoes, lima beans, and corn. Return to a boil. Remove pig's feet, debone, and return meat to pot. Reduce heat, cover, and simmer for about 30 minutes.

—Vernell, GEORGIA

Ham, Potato, and Leek Soup

Makes 4 to 6 Servings

2 tablespoons olive oil

1 medium onion, chopped

2 small leeks, halved lengthwise and thinly sliced
   with dark green leaves discarded

2 carrots, peeled and roughly diced

¾ cup frozen green peas

1 pound red potatoes, roughly diced

1 pound ham, cubed

1 quart chicken broth

1 teaspoon dried thyme

Salt, to taste

Pepper, to taste

Heat olive oil in a Dutch oven. Add onion and sauté until slightly softened, about 2 minutes. Add leeks, carrots, peas, potatoes, ham, chicken broth, and thyme. Partially cover, and simmer over medium-low heat until vegetables are tender, about 20 minutes. Add salt and pepper to taste. Serve hot. If you don't have potatoes on hand when planning to make this soup, 2 (16-ounce) cans of white beans or hominy may be substituted for the potatoes.

—*Rick,* MISSISSIPPI

Turtle Soup

Makes 6 Servings

2 pounds turtle meat
1 gallon water
1 bay leaf
2 cloves garlic
1 teaspoon lemon juice
Salt, to taste
Pepper, to taste
1 cup vegetable oil
1 cup flour
1 cup onions, chopped
2 stalks celery, finely chopped
4 tablespoons tomato paste
6 eggs, boiled and halved
6 tablespoons sherry

Combine turtle meat and 1 gallon of water in a large stockpot and bring to a boil. Add bay leaf, garlic, lemon juice, salt, and pepper. Reduce heat to medium and simmer until turtle meat is tender, approximately 1½–2 hours.

In an iron skillet, combine oil and flour to make a roux. See roux recipe on page 170. Remove from heat. Add onions, celery, and tomato paste, stirring constantly. Add roux/vegetable mixture to boiled turtle meat and cook another 45 minutes, or until soup is desired thickness. When ready to serve, place a halved boiled egg and a tablespoon of sherry in each bowl before ladling the soup.

—*Diane,* LOUISIANA

Creole Bouillabaisse

Makes 10 Servings

2 tablespoons butter
2 tablespoons olive oil
¼ cup flour
1 cup onions, chopped
½ cup celery, chopped
1 clove garlic, minced
4 cups fish or chicken stock
1 (28-ounce) can tomatoes, diced
½ cup dry white wine
2 tablespoons parsley, chopped
1 tablespoon lemon juice
1 bay leaf
½ teaspoon salt
⅛ teaspoon cayenne pepper
¼ teaspoon saffron (optional)
1 pound fresh fish fillets, cut into 1½-inch chunks
1 cup fresh oysters, shelled
½ pound shrimp, peeled and deveined

In a large pot, make a roux using the butter, olive oil, and flour. See roux recipe on page 170. Add the onion, celery, and garlic, stirring constantly. Gradually add the fish or chicken stock. Stir in remaining ingredients except fish, oysters, and shrimp. Bring to a boil and simmer for 10 minutes. Add fish and simmer 10 additional minutes. Add shrimp and oysters and cook 5 minutes more. Serve hot.

—*Jack,* LOUISIANA

Jack's Clam Chowder

*This chowder is best when stored in the refrigerator
for 1 to 2 days before serving. It also freezes well.*

Makes 8 to 10 Servings

1 stick (½ cup) butter
½ cup plus 3 tablespoons flour
1 teaspoon salt
½ teaspoon red cayenne pepper
3 cups cream
6 (6.5-ounce) cans clams, with juice
2 medium carrots, finely chopped
2 medium onions, finely chopped
2 teaspoons Italian seasoning
2 teaspoons parsley
½ teaspoon pepper
16 ounces sour cream

Melt the butter in a large pan. Add flour, salt, red pepper, and cream.
Stir until smooth. Add clams, clam juice, carrots, and onions; stir.
Add Italian seasoning, parsley, pepper, and sour cream. Simmer for
1 hour over low heat. Serve hot.

—*Jack,* KENTUCKY

*Chowder breathes reassurance.
It steams consolation.*

—CLEMENTINE PADDLEFORD

Shrimp, Crab, and Corn Chowder

Makes 8 Servings

6 cups low sodium chicken broth

2 pounds shrimp, peeled, deveined, and chopped; shells reserved

1 cup white wine

3 ears corn, kernels removed, kernels and cobs reserved

3 strips bacon, diced

2 large carrots, peeled and diced

1 large yellow onion, finely chopped

3 celery stalks, diced

2½ cups heavy cream

2 medium potatoes, diced

1 pound crabmeat

Salt, to taste

Pepper, to taste

1 teaspoon fresh thyme, chopped

1 teaspoon fresh chives, chopped

French bread and butter, for serving

In a large pot, combine chicken broth, shrimp shells, wine, and corncobs. Simmer for about 25 minutes. Liquid should be reduced to about 3½ cups. In a Dutch oven over medium heat, sauté diced bacon until crisp. Add carrots, onions, celery, and corn kernels. Cook, stirring frequently, until vegetables are tender, about 4 minutes. Pour shell/cob mixture through a strainer held over the Dutch oven to add the shell/cob liquid to bacon and vegetables. Add cream and bring to simmer. Stir in potatoes, reduce heat, and cook until potatoes are tender, about 15–18 minutes. Gently stir in shrimp, crabmeat, salt, pepper, thyme, and chives. Cook until heated through, about 3–4 minutes. Adjust seasonings to taste. Serve with French bread and butter. Can be made the day before serving and refrigerated overnight to allow flavors to blend.

—*Frances*, ALABAMA

Tuesdays Together Gumbo

For a Crowd

Makes 20 to 25 Servings

3 quarts water
3 pounds chicken, cut into bite-size pieces
1 bunch celery, chopped
1 onion, quartered
$\frac{1}{3}$ cup cooking oil
$\frac{1}{2}$ cup flour
1 pound frozen cut okra
1 cup onion, chopped
1 cup celery, chopped
1 (46-ounce) can V-8™ juice
$\frac{1}{2}$ pound ham, cooked and cubed
2 (16-ounce) cans tomatoes
1 pound smoked sausage, sliced
2 pounds shrimp, shells discarded
Salt, to taste
Pepper, to taste
Cooked rice, for serving

In a large pot, bring water to a boil. Add the chicken, chopped celery bunch, and quartered onion. Simmer 30 minutes or until chicken is cooked through and vegetables are tender. In a separate pot, use the oil and flour to make a roux. See roux recipe on page 170. Add okra, chopped onion, and 1 cup chopped celery to roux and cook for 15 minutes. Add the V-8™ juice, ham, tomatoes, sausage, and the entire contents of the other pot and bring to a simmer. Add shrimp and simmer until shrimp turn pink, about 3 minutes. Season to taste. Serve over rice.

—*Don*, ARKANSAS

Gumbo New Orleans Style

Makes 25 to 30 Servings

For a Crowd

6 cups water

1 pound chicken gizzards, chopped

2 tablespoons seasoned salt

2 teaspoons parsley flakes

1 teaspoon paprika

Dash ground red pepper

1½ cups green bell pepper, chopped

1 cup onion, chopped

5 cloves garlic, finely chopped

1 teaspoon onion powder

1 teaspoon garlic powder

1 teaspoon dried thyme

1 teaspoon black pepper

1 cup flour

½ cup vegetable oil

1 pound frozen chopped okra

6 pounds crabmeat

2 pounds fresh, uncooked shrimp, peeled and deveined

2 pounds uncooked turkey or beef sausage links,
    cut into 1-inch pieces

1 (8-ounce) can regular or smoked oysters, drained

Hot cooked rice, for serving

In a large pot, bring water to a boil. Add gizzards, seasoned salt, parsley, paprika, red pepper, green pepper, onion, garlic, onion powder, garlic powder, thyme, and black pepper. Reduce heat to medium-low and simmer for 1 hour. In a small pot, use flour and oil to make a roux. See roux recipe on page 170. Add the roux to the gizzards and stir until blended. Stir in okra, crabmeat, shrimp, sausage, and oysters; bring to a boil. Reduce heat and simmer 5–10 minutes, or until shrimp are pink and firm. Serve hot over rice.

—*Irma,* GEORGIA

Alligator Chili
(Chili with a Bite)

Makes 15 Servings

DAY 1:

2–3 pounds alligator tail meat

1½ cups red wine

1 clove garlic, minced

DAY 2:

2 tablespoons olive oil

1 bell pepper, finely chopped

1 large red onion, finely chopped

4 cloves garlic, minced

⅛ teaspoon ground allspice

⅛ teaspoon ground cloves

½ teaspoon ground cumin

¼ teaspoon ground coriander

1 teaspoon salt

½ teaspoon oregano

1 tablespoon parsley, minced

1 cup chicken broth

1 (10- or 12-ounce) can beer

1 (8–12 ounce) can mild green chiles, chopped

1 (8-ounce) can tomato sauce

1 (28-ounce) can tomatoes, chopped, juice reserved

1 (15-ounce) can pinto beans

1 (15-ounce) can pinto beans with jalapeños

2 tablespoons molasses

1½ cup red wine

Day 1: Prepare alligator meat by trimming all of the fat, which contains a "gamey" taste. Dice meat into ½-inch pieces. Place the meat in a medium bowl and add wine and garlic. Cover and marinate overnight.

Day 2: Drain alligator meat, reserving marinade. Heat olive oil in a heavy 5-quart pot. Cook meat over medium-high heat until browned, about 10 minutes. Remove browned meat and place in a bowl, leaving oil and liquids in the pot. Reduce heat to medium. Add bell pepper, onion, and garlic to the pot and sauté until soft. Add reserved liquid marinade, allspice, clove, cumin, coriander, salt, oregano, and parsley. Cover and simmer for 10 minutes. Add meat, chicken broth, beer, chiles, tomato sauce, chopped tomatoes, tomato liquid, beans, molasses, and red wine. Cover and simmer for 1 hour, stirring occasionally. Serve hot.

—*Wade*, LOUISIANA

Venison Chili

Makes 15 to 20 Servings

2 tablespoons canola oil, divided
2 pounds venison, cut into ½-inch cubes
1 (6-ounce) can tomato paste
4 large sweet onions, chopped
1 (16-ounce) can jalapeño peppers, diced
1 tablespoon chili powder
1 tablespoon cayenne pepper
2 pounds fresh tomatoes, diced
1 (48-ounce) can tomato sauce
2 (16-ounce) cans dark red kidney beans, liquid reserved
3 tablespoons chili powder
3 tablespoons cayenne pepper
3 tablespoons red pepper flakes
2 tablespoons freshly ground black pepper
2 tablespoons Tabasco™ sauce
1 tablespoon salt
2 (12-ounce) cans dark beer
3 (1-ounce) squares unsweetened chocolate

Heat 1 tablespoon of the canola oil in a large frying pan over medium-high heat. Cook the venison until it is slightly browned. While the meat is browning, slowly stir in the can of tomato paste. The tomato paste will turn dark and will provide a smoky flavor.

Remove the meat from the frying pan and place into an 8-quart stockpot over low heat. Add 1 tablespoon of canola oil to the frying pan used to brown the venison. Add the onions, jalapeño peppers, 1 tablespoon of chili powder, and 1 tablespoon of cayenne pepper. Stir to coat the onions and peppers with the spices. Sauté until the onions are almost translucent.

Remove the onions and peppers from the frying pan and pour them on top of the meat in the stockpot; stir. Add remaining ingredients, except the chocolate, to the stockpot. Stir with a heavy spoon and mix thoroughly. Bring the mixture in the stockpot to a low boil. Add the chocolate and stir until chocolate starts to melt. Once the chocolate has melted, reduce the heat to low, and let the chili simmer for at least 3 hours.

—*Al*, SOUTH CAROLINA

Fish Stew

This stew can be frozen for later use.
Makes 14 Servings

1 (28-ounce) can tomatoes
2 (14.5-ounce) cans stewed Italian-style tomatoes
2 (15-ounce) cans tomato sauce
1 large onion, chopped
4–5 carrots, thinly sliced
4–5 medium potatoes, diced
3–4 stalks celery, sliced
3 teaspoons Cajun seasoning
Salt, to taste
Pepper, to taste
1–2 cups water
1 pound shelled shrimp
1 pound boneless fish such as orange roughy,
    cut into small chunks
Flavored rice, cooked (optional)

In a large pot, bring tomatoes and tomato sauce to a boil, stirring occasionally. Add onion, carrots, potatoes, celery, Cajun seasoning, salt, and pepper. Reduce heat and simmer until vegetables are tender, about 20 minutes. Thin to desired consistency with water. Add shrimp and fish and cook until done, about 10 minutes. If desired, stir in some cooked, flavored rice for a heartier soup.

—*Frances,* SOUTH CAROLINA

Shem Creek Shrimp Boil
(Frogmore Stew)

Makes 10 Servings

Shrimp seasoning, to taste
1 pound new potatoes
1 pound smoked sausage, cut into 1-inch pieces
3 ears of corn on cob, husked, cleaned, and quartered
1 pound fresh shrimp, peeled and deveined
Cocktail sauce, butter, and sour cream, for serving

Fill a large pot half-full with water. Add shrimp seasoning to taste and bring to a boil. Add potatoes and sausage; cook for about 10 minutes. Add the corn; cook for another 5 minutes. Add more water as needed. When potatoes, sausage, and corn are almost cooked through, add shrimp and cook until they are pink and floating, about 3 minutes. Remove from heat. Carefully pour contents of pot into a colander to drain water. Serve on a platter with cocktail sauce, butter, and sour cream.

—*Rial*, SOUTH CAROLINA

Potato was deep in the dark under ground,

Tomato, above in the light;

The little Tomato was ruddy and round,

The little Potato was white.

And redder and redder she rounded above,

And paler and paler he grew.

And neither suspected a mutual love,

Till they met in a Brunswick stew.

—JOHN BANISTER TABB (1845–1909)

Georgia humorist Ray Blount Jr. claims **"Brunswick stew is what happens when small mammals carrying ears of corn fall into barbeque pits."** Virginia claims Brunswick stew originated in 1828 in Brunswick County, Virginia. It is said that Virginia state legislator Dr. Creed Haskins was on a hunting trip with friends. His camp cook, "Uncle" Jimmy Matthews, prepared a pot of squirrel stew thickened with onions and stale bread to nourish the hunters upon their return to camp. The stew proved so popular with the hunting party that Haskins later engaged Matthews to cook up a giant pot of squirrel stew for an Andrew Jackson political rally.

Ingredient substitutions and additions to the original recipe have evolved. Today, Brunswick stew is a thick, catch-all concoction containing rabbit or chicken, onions, corn, and a variety of other vegetables.

Virginia Brunswick Stew

This stew is especially tasty when cooked outside over a wood fire. The consistency is more like soup than thick stew.

Makes 15 Servings

DAY 1:
5 pounds fresh chicken, squirrel, or other game meat
¼ pound fatback or streaked bacon
Dash cayenne pepper
1 medium white onion

DAY 2:
1 (16-ounce) can butter beans
1 (8-ounce) can stewed tomatoes
5 ears corn, kernels cut from cob and cob discarded
1 cup fresh cabbage, finely sliced
1 cup frozen black-eyed peas
Freshly ground black pepper, for rubbing
Salt, for rubbing

Day 1: Combine chicken, fatback, cayenne pepper, and onion in a large pot. Cover with water and bring to a boil. Reduce heat to a simmer and cook until chicken is tender and cooked through. Cool. Remove chicken from pot. Remove skin from the chicken and remove chicken from the bones. Discard skin and bones. Discard fatback. Strain the broth and reserve broth. Store chicken with onion in a covered container. Store broth in a separate covered container. Refrigerate both containers overnight.

Day 2: Skim fat from broth and pour skimmed broth into a large pot. Rub chicken with salt and pepper and cut it into quarter-size chunks. Add chicken, onion, butter beans, tomatoes, corn, cabbage, and black-eyed peas to the pot of broth. Simmer over low to medium-low heat until vegetables are tender.

—*Pastor,* SOUTH CAROLINA

Soup for a Crowd

Makes 20 Servings

1 gallon chicken stock
½ cup flour
½ stick (¼ cup) margarine
2 teaspoons curry powder
1–1½ cups onions, finely diced
1 cup celery, finely diced
1 cup carrots, finely diced
2¼ cups Granny Smith apples, peeled and diced
1 cup shredded coconut
½ teaspoon ground mace
4½ tablespoons salt
1 tablespoon Accent™
1½ quarts hot milk

Heat the chicken stock in a large saucepan over medium-low heat. In a large soup pot, make a roux using the flour and margarine. See roux recipe on page 170. Add curry powder and the hot stock to the finished roux. Stir constantly until sauce is thickened and smooth, about 30 minutes. Add onions, celery, and carrots to sauce and simmer until tender, about 40 minutes. Add apples, coconut, mace, salt, and Accent.™ Simmer 20 minutes longer. Add hot milk; remove from heat and blend well. Taste and add seasonings, if desired. Serve hot.

—*Dana*, ALABAMA

Kentucky Hot Browns

Makes 4 to 6 Sandwiches

SAUCE:
4 ounces butter
6 tablespoons flour
3–3½ cups milk
6 tablespoons Parmesan cheese, grated
1 egg, beaten
Salt, to taste
Pepper, to taste

HOT BROWNS:
4–6 slices bread, toasted
18 ounces roasted turkey, sliced
Parmesan cheese, for garnish
1 tomato, sliced
8–12 strips bacon, fried

Sauce: In a medium sauce pan, make a roux using the butter and flour. See page 170 for roux recipe. Whisk milk and Parmesan cheese into the finished roux. Carefully add egg to thicken sauce. Do not allow sauce to boil. Cook over medium-low heat, stirring often until sauce is desired thickness. Remove from heat. Add salt and pepper, to taste.

Hot Browns: Preheat oven to "broil." For each Hot Brown, place a slice of toast on an ovenproof plate. Cover toast with slices of turkey. Pour a generous amount of sauce over the turkey and the toast. Sprinkle with additional cheese and broil until sauce is speckled brown and bubbly, about 5 minutes. Remove from broiler and add tomato slices. Cross 2 strips of bacon on top and serve immediately. Take care when handling the hot plate.

—*LauraLee*, KENTUCKY

Muffuletta

This sandwich is traditionally made with "muffuletta," a type of Sicilian bread. Muffuletta is baked as a round loaf about 10 inches across. The bread's texture is sturdy. If you can't find muffuletta at your local bakery, substitute a large round loaf of Italian bread.

Makes 8 Sandwiches

OLIVE SALAD:
5 ounces green olives, drained and minced
6 ounces black olives, drained and diced
1 teaspoon dried basil
2 teaspoons dried oregano
1 teaspoon garlic powder
1 tablespoon red onion, chopped
¼ cup olive oil
Dash red wine vinegar

SANDWICHES:
1 loaf of muffuletta bread
¼ pound salami, sliced
½ pound ham, sliced
½ pound provolone cheese, sliced
2 tablespoons butter, melted

Olive salad: Combine all salad ingredients in a small bowl; stir to mix. Cover and refrigerate overnight.

Sandwiches: Preheat oven to 350°F. Slice bread lengthwise into 3 layers. Set top and middle layers aside. Place bottom layer on cookie sheet and spread half of the olive salad onto the bread layer. Add half of the meat and half of the cheese. Place middle bread layer on top and cover with the rest of the olive salad, meat, and cheese. Place the last bread layer on the sandwich and brush with melted butter. Cover with aluminum foil. Bake for 1 hour or until sandwich is heated through and the cheese is melted. Cut into pie-like wedges to serve.

—*Regina*, KENTUCKY

Pistolettes

Makes 6 Sandwiches

6 hard French rolls
10 ounces broccoli, chopped
8 ounces Velveeta™ cheese
1 pound bulk sausage, cooked and drained
3 tablespoons butter, melted

Preheat oven to 400°F. Cut off one end of each roll and scoop out the bread in the center to create a hollow space in each roll. Steam the broccoli until it turns vibrant green, no more than 5 minutes. Remove from heat and set aside. In a medium saucepan, melt the cheese; stir the broccoli and cooked sausage into the melted cheese. Carefully fill the hollowed-out rolls with the mixture. Place the ends of the rolls back on top and brush them with melted butter. Bake for 15–20 minutes or until very golden brown.

—*Lou*, ALABAMA

Egg Salad Sandwiches

For a Crowd

Makes 90 Sandwiches

7 dozen eggs	Salt, to taste
9 ounces prepared mustard	Pepper, to taste
½ gallon mayonnaise	8 large loaves thin-sliced bread

When boiling this many eggs, it's a good idea to use two large pots. Fill the pots with water and place the eggs in the pots. Bring the water to a boil and boil for 5–7 minutes. Rinse the eggs with cold water and have a good time peeling them—it's fun! Place the eggs in a food processor and chop them nice and small. Unless you have a jumbo-sized processor, don't try to process all of the eggs at once. In a large bowl, mix the mustard and mayonnaise. Add eggs, salt, and pepper; stir gently. Serve the egg salad in a big bowl. Place loaves of bread on the table, set out some spoons and knives, and folks will be equipped to make their own sandwiches.

—*Betty*, SOUTH CAROLINA

Nonnie's Sloppy Joes

Makes 8 Sandwiches

2 pounds ground beef
1 cup ketchup
½ cup sugar
2 tablespoons white vinegar
2 tablespoons Worcestershire sauce
2 tablespoons lemon juice
1½ teaspoons onion, minced
1 teaspoon ground red pepper
8 hamburger buns, for serving

In a large skillet, brown ground beef; drain. Add remaining ingredients to the browned ground beef; stir to combine. Cook until heated through. Serve on hamburger buns.

—*Constance Jane*, KENTUCKY

Pimento Cheese Sandwiches

For a Crowd

Makes 90 Sandwiches

8 pounds sharp cheese, shredded
2 (24-ounce) cans chopped pimentos, drained
3–4 dashes Worcestershire sauce
½ gallon mayonnaise
8 large loaves thin-sliced bread

In a large bowl, combine all ingredients except the bread and mix well. Spread mixture between two slices of bread.

—*Betty*, SOUTH CAROLINA

Entrées and Sauces

Appetite is the best sauce.

—FRENCH PROVERB

Quiche Lorraine

Makes 4 Servings

1 tablespoon butter, softened
1 9-inch deep-dish pie shell, unbaked and chilled
12 strips bacon, fried crisp and crumbled
1 cup Swiss cheese, shredded
4 eggs, lightly beaten
2 cups heavy cream
¾ teaspoon salt
Pinch of nutmeg
Pinch of sugar
Pinch of cayenne pepper

Preheat oven to 425°F. Spread butter on interior surface of pie shell. Sprinkle cooked and crumbled bacon and shredded cheese in pie shell. In a small bowl, combine lightly beaten eggs, cream, and seasonings. Beat until well mixed. Pour mixture on top of bacon and cheese.

Bake for 15 minutes at 425°F. Remove quiche from oven. Reduce oven temperature to 300°F. Allow quiche to stand for 15 minutes. Return quiche to oven and bake for 40 additional minutes.

—*Louise*, LOUISIANA

Basic Frittata

Makes 4 Servings

8 eggs
3 tablespoons Parmesan cheese, grated,
    plus more for topping
2 tablespoons fresh parsley or fresh basil,
    chopped, or 1 teaspoon dried thyme
Ground nutmeg, to taste
3 slices bacon, cut into ½-inch pieces or
    6 ounces of ground sausage, crumbled
1 small onion, diced
6 button mushrooms, diced
1 medium clove garlic, minced

Preheat oven to 400°F. In a large bowl, lightly beat eggs with cheese, herb of choice, salt, pepper, and nutmeg. Set aside.

Fry bacon or sausage in an ovenproof skillet until lightly browned. Add mushrooms and onions. Sauté for about 6 minutes. Season with salt and pepper. Reduce heat to low, add garlic, and cook about 1 minute longer. Spread skillet ingredients evenly in the bottom of pan, pour egg mixture on top of ingredients in skillet, and sprinkle with additional cheese. Do not stir. Cook until set around the edges, about 1 minute.

Place pan in oven, and bake about 10–12 minutes until puffed and set. Slice and serve hot.

—Rick, MISSISSIPPI

Leek Lasagna

Makes 4 Servings

5 medium leeks, washed and sliced

3 tablespoons butter, divided

2 tablespoons flour

3 cups milk

Salt, to taste

Pepper, to taste

1 (1-pound) package lasagna noodles,
    cooked and drained

6 slices ham, cut into small pieces

2 cups mozzarella cheese, grated

Preheat oven to 350°F. Place the leeks and 1 tablespoon of butter in a large pot. Add enough water to cover leeks and cook over medium-high heat for 15 minutes. While leeks are cooking, melt 2 tablespoons butter in a saucepan over low heat. Add flour and stir for 2 minutes. Do not brown. Gradually stir in milk. Continue to cook, stirring constantly, until sauce thickens. Add salt and pepper, to taste. Remove from heat and set aside. Pour a small amount of the white sauce into a 9x13-inch casserole dish. Add a layer of lasagna noodles. Cover the noodles with half of the leeks, ham, white sauce, and cheese. Add a second layer of noodles, leeks, ham, white sauce, and cheese. Bake for 30 minutes.

—Cathy, MISSISSIPPI

Once a southern Appalachian delicacy, ramps have now immigrated to the wild foods section of gourmet food stores across the country. Ramps are wild leeks and taste sweet, with a hint of garlic, when cooked. Eaten raw, expect a strong, pungent odor of onion and garlic. Fresh ramps are only available in the springtime. According to southern regional folklore, eating fresh ramps is akin to drinking a revitalizing tonic. A Native American legend recalls the power of ramps to cleanse the blood.

Holiday Brunch Casserole

Makes 6 Servings

1 pound sausage, cooked, drained, and crumbled
4 cups day-old bread, cubed
2 cups sharp Cheddar cheese, shredded
1 teaspoon dry mustard
¼ teaspoon onion powder
10 eggs, lightly beaten
4 cups milk
1 teaspoon salt
Pepper, to taste

Place bread in well-buttered 9x13-inch baking dish. Sprinkle cheese on top of bread. In a large bowl, mix dry mustard, onion powder, eggs, milk, salt, and pepper. Pour mixture on top of bread and cheese in baking dish; sprinkle cooked sausage on top. Cover and refrigerate overnight.

Preheat oven to 325°F. Bake uncovered for about 1 hour. Place aluminum foil loosely over casserole if the top begins to brown too quickly. Serve hot.

—*Frankie and Judi,* NORTH CAROLINA

Thelma June's Pancake Supper

For a Crowd

Makes 50 Pancakes

Serve hot with butter, maple-flavored syrup, and any fruit you can convince the kids to spend some time picking. Throw in a few gallons of OJ and a few gallons of milk for drinking and you've got yourself a Thelma June supper.

8 cups Bisquick™
1⅓ cups sour cream
3 cups milk
¼ cup brown sugar, packed
8 eggs, beaten
Butter, for serving
Maple-flavored syrup, for serving

If you plan to fry the pancakes on a griddle, preheat the griddle to 375°F. If you're not using a griddle, you'll want as many pans going as you can handle. You know the pans are hot enough when a drop of water sprinkled on the pan does a little dance before disappearing. In a large bowl, combine Bisquick,™ sour cream, milk, brown sugar, and beaten eggs. Stir until well mixed. Pour ¼ cup of batter onto a griddle or into a pan for each pancake. Cook until the bottom is golden, the edges are dry, and little bubbles start to form on the surface. Flip the pancake over and cook a little bit longer until both sides are golden.

—*Thelma June,* ALABAMA

Grilled White Fish in Lemon Sauce

Makes 2 Servings

Halibut, orange roughy, snapper, or tilapia would be good choices for the fish in this dish.

2 tablespoons butter
1 large red onion, chopped
4–5 cloves garlic, thinly sliced
1 teaspoon salt
½–1 tablespoon fresh chives, chopped
2 lemons, zest from both lemons and
    juice from ½ lemon reserved
½ teaspoon fresh dill, chopped
¼–½ cup white wine
2 tablespoons olive oil
1 pound white fish, divided into 2 pieces

Prepare grill for cooking over hot coals. Melt butter in a saucepan; add onion and garlic and sauté until onion is translucent. Add the salt, chives, lemon zest, lemon juice, dill, and wine. Cook until liquid is reduced by a third. Add olive oil and remove from heat.

Place 2 large squares of aluminum foil on a flat surface. Put a tablespoonful of sauce and a piece of fish into the center of each square. Cover fish with additional sauce. Tightly wrap foil around fish. Grill over high heat for about 3 minutes.

—*Fred,* NORTH CAROLINA

Island-Style Baked Fish

Makes 6 Servings

2 pounds grouper or snapper fillets
2 onions, thinly sliced
2 tomatoes, sliced
½ cup black olives, sliced
1 cup dry white wine
1 lemon, sliced
1 lime, sliced
1 orange, sliced

Preheat oven to 375°F. Place fish in a large baking dish. Layer with onions, tomatoes, and olives. Pour wine over fish and vegetables. Cover and bake until fish flakes easily, about 30 minutes. Arrange lemon, lime, and orange slices in the center of each plate. Top the fruit with a serving of fish and vegetables.

—*Beverly,* SOUTH CAROLINA

> *I must confess that fishing*
> *has never been a great passion of mine,*
> *as it seems to require more patience*
> *than I normally have on hand.*
> *But cooking and eating fish …*
> *Well, that's a different story.*
>
> —WOLFGANG PUCK

Macadamia Nut-Breaded Fish with Guava Lime Sauce

Makes 6 Servings

FISH:

2½ cups flour, plus more for dusting

2 cups water

2 cups seasoned breadcrumbs

½ cup macadamia nuts, finely chopped

6 fish fillets, skinless

¼ cup vegetable oil

SAUCE:

¾ cup guava purée

1 lime, juiced

½ cup white wine

¾ cup heavy cream

1 cup butter

Salt, to taste

Pepper, to taste

Fish: In a medium bowl, combine flour and water; mix until a smooth batter-like consistency. In a separate bowl, combine breadcrumbs and nuts. One by one, lightly dust fillets with flour, dip in the flour/water mixture, and roll fillets in the nut mixture. Heat the oil in a skillet and fry fish until browned on both sides, turning only once. If necessary, add more oil to the skillet.

Sauce: In a small saucepan, combine guava purée, lime juice, and white wine. Simmer until liquid is reduced by half. Add heavy cream and reduce liquid again by half. Add butter, a tablespoon at a time, stirring constantly. As soon as butter is incorporated, remove from heat, and season with salt and pepper. Ladle sauce over fish and serve.

—*Terri*, VIRGINIA

Southern Catfish

Makes 8 Servings

Peanut oil, for frying
1⅓ cup cornmeal
⅔ cup flour
1 tablespoon salt
1 teaspoon ground red pepper
1 cup buttermilk
4 pounds catfish, dressed

In a deep skillet, heat peanut oil to 375°F. In a large bowl, add cornmeal, flour, salt, and pepper; whisk to combine. Pour buttermilk into a small bowl. Dip fish in the buttermilk and dredge in the cornmeal mixture. Fry fish for 3–4 minutes per side. Fish is cooked through when the meat flakes easily off the bones.

—*Pam,* KENTUCKY

Pecan Dijon Baked Catfish

Makes 4 Servings

4 catfish fillets
Salt and pepper, to taste
¼ cup (4 tablespoons) Dijon mustard
1 stick (½ cup) butter, melted
½ cup dry breadcrumbs
½ cup pecans, ground

Preheat oven to 475°F. Rinse catfish, pat dry, and place rounded side up on a greased baking sheet. Season to taste with salt and pepper. Brush each fillet with 1 tablespoon of mustard. In a small bowl, combine melted butter, breadcrumbs, and pecans. Spread ¼ cup of mixture over each fillet. Press firmly onto surface of fish to coat. Spray each fillet with non-stick cooking spray. Bake for 13–15 minutes or until fish flakes easily.

—*Linda*, MISSISSIPPI

George Washington's pockets are said to have often contained a cache of pecans available for impromptu snacking. He called them his "Mississippi nuts." Washington had planted several pecan trees on the grounds of his Mount Vernon home in 1775. He received these trees as a gift from a man in Monticello. This Monticello resident with horticultural interests was Thomas Jefferson and he had transplanted his trees from the Mississippi Valley. Three of the pecan trees presented to George Washington in 1775 continue to grow on the Mount Vernon property today.

Pecan trees grow to over one hundred feet tall and live to be over a thousand years old.

Catfish Parmesan

Makes 6 Servings

2 cups dry breadcrumbs
¾ cup Parmesan cheese
¼ cup parsley, chopped
1 teaspoon paprika
½ teaspoon oregano
¼ teaspoon basil
2 teaspoons salt
½ teaspoon pepper
6 catfish fillets
¾ cup butter, melted
Lemon wedges, for garnish

Preheat oven to 375°F. In a large bowl, combine breadcrumbs, cheese, parsley, paprika, oregano, basil, salt, and pepper. Dip catfish in melted butter and dredge in crumb mixture. Arrange fish in a well-greased 9x13-inch baking dish. Bake for about 15 minutes or until fish flakes easily. Garnish with lemon wedges and serve hot.

—*Anita*, MISSISSIPPI

If I go down for anything in history,
I would like to be known
as the person who convinced
the American people that catfish is one
of the finest eating fishes in the world.

—WILLARD SCOTT

Baked Salmon with Pecan Crunch Coating

Makes 4 Servings

4 (4–6 ounce) salmon fillets
⅛ teaspoon salt
⅛ teaspoon pepper
2 tablespoons Dijon mustard
2 tablespoons butter, melted
1½ tablespoons honey
¼ cup soft breadcrumbs
¼ cup pecans, finely chopped
2 teaspoons fresh parsley, chopped

Preheat oven and a lightly oiled 13x9-inch pan to 450°F. Sprinkle salmon with salt and pepper. In a small bowl, combine mustard, butter, and honey; spread mixture on top of salmon, skin side down. In a separate small bowl, combine breadcrumbs, pecans, and chopped parsley; spoon mixture evenly over top of each fillet. Carefully place prepared salmon in the preheated baking pan. Bake until the fish flake easily, about 10 minutes. Serve immediately.

—*Kim,* SOUTH CAROLINA

Salmon with Dill Sauce

Makes 4 Servings

2 tablespoons butter
¼ cup green onions, sliced
1 (14-ounce) can chicken broth
Juice of 1 lemon
1 tablespoon dried dill weed
Black pepper, coarsely ground, to taste
2 (1-pound) salmon fillets
2 tablespoons Dijon mustard
¼ cup sour cream

Melt butter in a large saucepan. Add onions; cook until translucent. Add chicken broth, lemon juice, dill, and black pepper. Bring to a boil, reduce heat to medium-low, and add salmon. Cover and poach 15 minutes, until fish turn opaque and are slightly firm. Transfer fish to platter; keep fillets warm. Bring broth to a boil. Allow broth to boil until liquid is reduced by half, 3–4 minutes. Reduce heat to low, stir in mustard and sour cream and cook until heated through. Pour sauce over fillets and serve.

—*Chris,* VIRGINIA

Grilled Honey-Balsamic Salmon

Makes 2 Servings

1½ tablespoons honey
1½ tablespoons Dijon mustard
1 tablespoon balsamic vinegar
¼ teaspoon pepper, coarsely ground
¼ teaspoon garlic salt
2 (6-ounce, ½-inch thick) salmon steaks

Prepare grill for cooking over medium-hot coals. In a small bowl, add honey, mustard, vinegar, pepper, and garlic salt; stir to combine. Brush surface of fish with mixture. Lightly spray the grill rack with non-stick cooking oil. Transfer fish to grill rack and cook, covered, until fish flake easily when tested with a fork, 2–3 minutes on each side. Serve immediately.

—*Sandy,* NORTH CAROLINA

Grilled Herbed Salmon

Makes 4 to 6 Servings

½ cup butter
$\frac{1}{3}$ cup lemon juice
2 tablespoons parsley, minced
1½ teaspoons soy sauce
1½ teaspoons Worcestershire sauce
1 teaspoon dried oregano
½ teaspoon garlic powder
¼ teaspoon salt
$\frac{1}{8}$ teaspoon pepper
1 salmon fillet (2½–3 pounds, and ¾-inch thick)

In a saucepan, combine all ingredients, with the exception of the salmon. Cook and stir over low heat until butter is melted. Set aside.

Coat grill rack with nonstick cooking spray. Prepare grill for cooking over medium-hot charcoal. Place salmon, skin side down, on grill and cook for 5 minutes. Baste fish with butter sauce frequently while grilling for 10–15 minutes longer or until salmon flakes easily with a fork.

—*Theria,* NORTH CAROLINA

Glazed Salmon with Stir-Fried Vegetables

Makes 4 Servings

4 (4-ounce) salmon fillets
¼ teaspoon salt
2 tablespoons olive oil plus more to grease broiler pan
¼ cup apple jelly
3 tablespoons rice wine vinegar
2 tablespoons water
1 tablespoon soy sauce
1 teaspoon cornstarch
1 teaspoon fresh dill, chopped
2 carrots, cut into thin strips
1 parsnip, cut into thin strips
1 red bell pepper, cut into thin strips
8 green onions, cut into thin strips

Place oven rack 6-inches from heat source and preheat oven to broil. Sprinkle salmon with salt. Place salmon on a lightly oiled broiler pan and broil until fish flake easily, 10–13 minutes.

In a small bowl, add jelly, vinegar, water, soy sauce, and cornstarch; whisk to combine. Add dill and stir.

Heat 2 tablespoons olive oil in a large skillet. Add carrots, parsnip, pepper, and onions. Cook, stirring often, until vegetables are just tender, about 3 minutes. Transfer vegetables to a serving plate. Pour jelly mixture into the skillet used to cook the vegetables. Cook, stirring constantly, until mixture is thickened, about 4 minutes.

Drizzle half of the sauce over the vegetables, place salmon on top of vegetables, and drizzle remaining sauce over salmon. Serve immediately.

—*Ann*, SOUTH CAROLINA

Irish Scallop Pie with Potato Crust

Makes 8 Servings

1 pound potatoes, cooked and sliced
5 tablespoons unsalted butter, divided
3 cloves garlic, thinly sliced, divided
6 scallions, chopped, greens reserved
1 pound button mushrooms
2 pounds of large sea scallops
2 tablespoons flour
1 cup light cream
4 tablespoons light sherry
2 tablespoons fresh parsley, chopped
½ cup milk, if needed, for creaming potatoes

Preheat oven to 350°F. Melt 3 tablespoons of butter in a skillet; add all but a half clove of garlic and sauté. Be careful not to brown the garlic. Add scallions, reserving the green portions, and sauté for 2 minutes. Add mushrooms and scallops and sauté for 2–3 minutes. Sprinkle mixture with flour, and stir well. Add cream slowly, stirring constantly until combined. Bring to a boil and stir in sherry. Remove pan from heat; set aside.

In a large bowl, combine cooked, sliced potatoes, 2 tablespoons of butter, remaining ½ clove of garlic, and scallion greens. Using an electric mixer, beat potatoes until creamy, adding milk, if necessary.

Pour scallop mixture into a deep-dish pie pan. Spoon potatoes evenly on top of the scallop mixture. Bake for 20 minutes or until potatoes are brown.

—*Laura*, MISSISSIPPI

Virginia Batter Crab Cakes

Makes 4 Servings

1 bread heel, crumbled
1 pound crab meat
2 tablespoons butter, melted
2 eggs, lightly beaten
2 teaspoons mayonnaise
2 teaspoons mustard
Vegetable oil, for browning
Flour, for dusting
Fresh parsley, for garnish
Lemon wedges, for garnish

Combine crumbled bread and crab meat in a medium bowl; toss lightly to mix. In a separate bowl, mix melted butter, lightly beaten eggs, mayonnaise, and mustard. Lightly fold into crab mixture using a fork. Shape into 6-8 patties. Spray a large non-stick skillet with cooking oil and place over medium-high heat. Add crab cakes and cook about 3 minutes on each side until just browned. Transfer to floured baking dish and lightly dust tops with flour to hold them together. Cover and steam for 3 minutes. Drain on paper towels. Sprinkle with fresh parsley and garnish with lemon wedges.

—*Janis*, MISSISSIPPI

Mardi Gras Pasta

Makes 6 Servings

2 tablespoons butter
3 cups whole kernel corn
2 quarts whipping cream
¾ cup tasso, thinly sliced
⅓ cup red bell pepper
⅓ cup yellow bell pepper
⅓ cup green bell pepper
1½ tablespoons Cajun seasoning
1½ cups chicken, cooked and diced
1½ cups crawfish tails
6 tablespoons water
2 tablespoons cornstarch
½ cup green onions
1½ tablespoons parsley
2¾ tablespoons Parmesan cheese
12 ounces pasta, cooked

Melt butter in large skillet. Add corn and whipping cream; simmer until thick. Add tasso and bell peppers and cook an additional 2 minutes. Stir in Cajun seasoning. Add chicken and crawfish tails. In a small bowl, combine water and cornstarch; whisk until smooth. Add to sauce. Remove from heat. Stir in green onions, parsley, and cheese. Serve over pasta.

—*Wayne*, LOUISIANA

> *Sadness and good food
> are incompatible.*
>
> —CHARLES SIMIC

Fettuccine with Crawfish and Asparagus Tips

*"Us" Cajuns turn Italian once a month
because we love this dish so much. I serve it with a green salad,
hot garlic bread, and a lil' wine, of course.*

Makes 8 Servings

1 tablespoon salt, plus salt for seasoning
3 tablespoons olive oil, divided
1 pound fettuccine (fresh, if possible)
6 garlic cloves, diced
1 bunch green onions, finely chopped
½ cup bell pepper, finely diced
4 cups crawfish or shrimp, uncooked
2 cups fresh asparagus tips, blanched
½ cup pimentos, finely diced
½ cup white wine
Juice from 1 lime
7 black peppercorns, ground or crushed
½ stick (¼ cup) butter, room temperature
Parsley, chopped, for garnish
Parmesan or Romano cheese, grated, to taste

Fill a large pot with water and bring to a boil. Add 1 tablespoon salt, 1 tablespoon olive oil, and pasta. Cook pasta 8–15 minutes if dry, 3–5 minutes if fresh.

Heat 2 tablespoons of olive oil in a large pan. Add garlic, green onions, and bell pepper; cook for 30 seconds. Add shellfish, asparagus tips, and pimentos and cook for another 30 seconds. Add wine, lime juice, and pepper. Season with salt, to taste. Cook for 2 minutes. Add butter and stir until sauce is creamy.

When pasta is al dente—firm, but not hard at the center— pour into a colander and drain. Transfer the drained pasta to the saucepan. Add the parsley and grated cheese, to taste. Toss. Serve immediately.

—*Jackie,* LOUISIANA

Crawfish in Heaven

Makes 4 Servings

1 gallon water
8 ounces angel hair pasta
1 tablespoon olive oil
1 medium white onion, finely chopped
2 cloves garlic, puréed
1 celery stalk, finely chopped
3 tablespoons butter
1 pound crawfish tails
½ bunch green onions, chopped
½–1 cup half & half
Salt and pepper, to taste
Red pepper, to taste
2 tablespoons pimentos, chopped
Parsley, chopped, to taste
3 tablespoons Parmesan cheese, grated
2 ounces white wine or sherry

In a large pot, bring a gallon of water to a boil. Add pasta and cook until al dente. Drain. Toss with olive oil to keep pasta from sticking. Set aside. Sauté onion, garlic, and celery in butter until onions are translucent. Add crawfish tails. Sauté 10 more minutes over low heat. Add green onions, half & half, salt, peppers, pimientos, parsley, Parmesan cheese, and wine; stir to mix. Cook 5 more minutes over low heat. Toss with pasta. Serve immediately.

—*Julie*, LOUISIANA

Crawfish or Shrimp Étouffée

Makes 8 Servings

2 teaspoons salt
½ teaspoon red pepper flakes
½ teaspoon ground black pepper
1 teaspoon dried basil
½ teaspoon dried thyme
7 tablespoons peanut oil
¾ cup flour
1 onion, chopped
1 cup green onions, chopped
½ cup celery, chopped
1 tablespoon garlic, minced
1 tablespoon lemon juice
3 cups chicken broth
½ cup (1 stick) butter
2 pounds crawfish or shrimp,
    or 1 pound of each, shelled
4 cups rice, cooked

In a small bowl, mix salt, red pepper flakes, black pepper, basil, and thyme. Set aside. Combine the oil and flour in a large pot and make a roux. See roux recipe on page 170. Add onion, green onions, celery, and garlic to the finished roux and sauté over low heat for 3 minutes. Add lemon juice. Add chicken broth, 1 cup at a time, mixing each cup of broth thoroughly with ingredients in pot before adding the next cup. Whisk sauce until thickened. Pour into large bowl and set aside. Melt butter in a large skillet over medium-high heat. Sauté shellfish for about 1½ minutes per side, or until pink and fully cooked. Toss cooked shellfish in sauce and serve hot over rice.

—*Janie*, ARKANSAS

Lobster Thermidor

Makes 4 to 6 Servings

4 (1-pound) lobsters
¼ cup butter, melted
2 tablespoons flour
½ teaspoon prepared mustard
½ teaspoon dried minced onion
1 teaspoon salt
Dash of pepper
1½ cups light cream
2 tablespoons sherry
¼ cup Cheddar cheese, shredded
Lemon wedges, for garnish

Steam or boil lobsters. Remove meat and reserve shells. Cube lobster meat.

Melt butter in double boiler. Stir in flour, mustard, onion, salt, pepper, and cream. Cook, stirring until thickened. Add cubed lobster and sherry; cook until heated through.

Set the oven temperature to broil. Place reserved shells in broiler pan. Fill shells with lobster mixture. Sprinkle with cheese and brown under broiler. Garnish with lemon wedges.

—*Isabel*, LOUISIANA

I'm not interested in dishes that take three minutes and have no cholesterol.

—JULIA CHILD

Rich Seafood Casserole

Makes 8 to 10 Servings

1½ cups dry white wine
¼ cup onion, chopped
¼ cup fresh parsley sprigs
1 teaspoon salt
4 tablespoons butter, divided
1½ pounds large shrimp, peeled and deveined
1 pound bay scallops
3 tablespoons butter
3 tablespoons flour
1 cup half & half
½ cup Swiss cheese, shredded
1 tablespoon lemon juice
¾ teaspoon lemon pepper
½ pound mushrooms, sliced
1 cup soft, whole wheat breadcrumbs
¼ cup Parmesan cheese, grated
¼ cup almonds, sliced
Cooked rice, for serving

Preheat oven to 350°F. In a Dutch oven, combine wine, onion, parsley, salt, and 1 tablespoon butter; bring to a boil. Add shrimp and scallops; cook until shrimp turn pink, 3–5 minutes. Drain, reserving ⅔ cup of broth. Set the seafood aside.

Melt 3 tablespoons butter in the Dutch oven; add flour, stirring until smooth. Cook 1 minute, stirring constantly. Gradually add half & half; cook, stirring constantly, until mixture is thick and bubbly. Add Swiss cheese and stir until cheese melts. Gradually stir in reserved ⅔ cup of broth, lemon juice, and lemon pepper. Stir in shrimp/scallop mixture and mushrooms.

Spoon mixture into lightly greased 11x7x1½-inch baking dish. Cover and bake for 40 minutes. Combine breadcrumbs, Parmesan cheese, and almonds; sprinkle over casserole. Bake, uncovered, for an additional 10 minutes. Let stand 10 minutes before serving. Serve over rice.

—*Craig*, NORTH CAROLINA

Spicy Shrimp and Tasso Gravy Over Creamy White Grits

Makes 15 Servings

GRITS:

12 cups chicken broth

4½ cups grits

1 cup heavy cream

Salt and pepper, to taste

TASSO GRAVY:

4 tablespoons butter

½ cup tasso, cut in 1-inch strips
   (You can substitute country ham)

½ cup flour

2 cups chicken broth, divided

2 tablespoons parsley,
   finely chopped

Salt and pepper, to taste

SHRIMP AND SAUSAGE:

½ pound spicy Italian sausage

1 tablespoon olive oil

2 pounds shrimp,
   peeled and deveined

1 cup chicken broth

2 tablespoons parsley,
   chopped

Additional chopped parsley,
   for garnish

Grits: In a large saucepan, add chicken broth and bring to a boil. Slowly stir in grits. Reduce heat to low and cook 20–25 minutes, stirring often. When the grits have absorbed all of the broth and are soft, stir in the heavy cream, salt, and pepper. Cook another 10 minutes. Set aside.

Preheat oven to 400°F for the sausage.

Tasso Gravy: Melt butter in a large saucepan. Add tasso and sauté for 1 minute, browning slightly. Add flour; stir until well combined. Add ¼ cup of chicken broth and stir until thick and smooth. Gradually add the remaining broth, stirring until broth thickens into gravy. Reduce heat to low and simmer for 15 minutes. Add parsley. Season with salt and pepper.

(continued on next page)

Shrimp and Sausage: Place sausage on a baking sheet. Bake on the oven's top rack for 10-15 minutes, until sausage is firm. Cut into bite-sized pieces. Heat olive oil in a large saucepan. Add cooked sausage and shrimp. Sauté until shrimp turn pink, no longer than 1 minute. Add 1 cup chicken broth, tasso gravy, and parsley. Bring to boil. Remove from heat. Spoon over grits and sprinkle with parsley. Serve immediately.

—Margaret, TENNESSEE

Beer-Boiled Shrimp

Makes 4 Servings

1 cup beer
2 tablespoons peanut oil
1½ tablespoons Worcestershire sauce
2 tablespoons parsley, chopped
1 clove garlic, minced
Salt, to taste
Pepper, to taste
⅛ teaspoon hot sauce
2 pounds large shrimp, peeled and deveined,
   tails intact

In a large bowl, combine beer, peanut oil, Worcestershire sauce, parsley, garlic, salt, pepper, and hot sauce. Add shrimp and toss well. Cover and refrigerate for 2–3 hours.

Spray broiler rack with non-stick cooking spray. Adjust broiler rack 4-inches from the heat. Preheat oven to broil. Thread shrimp on skewers and place on broiler rack. Broil 3–4 minutes. Turn skewers over and broil shrimp until pink and cooked through, 1–2 more minutes.

—Wayne, LOUISIANA

Shrimp and Cheese Grits

Makes 4 Servings

GRITS:
4 cups water
1 teaspoon salt
1 cup instant grits
1 stick (½ cup) butter, melted
8 ounces mild Cheddar cheese, shredded
½ teaspoon garlic powder
3 eggs
¾ cup cream

SHRIMP SAUCE:
1 stick (½ cup) butter, divided
¾ cup onions, diced
15–20 large shrimp, cleaned, peeled and deveined
2 teaspoons herbes de Provence
2 teaspoons Cajun seasoning

GARNISH:
8 slices bacon, cooked crisp and diced
1 small bunch fresh parsley, minced
1 lemon, sliced into wedges

Grits: Preheat oven to 300°F. Grease a 2-quart casserole; set aside. In a medium saucepan, bring water to a boil; add salt and grits. Cook 3 minutes, stirring constantly. Remove from heat and stir in melted butter, cheese, and garlic powder; set aside. In a medium bowl, beat the eggs and cream until blended; add to grits and stir to combine. Pour grits into casserole and bake for 1 hour. While grits are baking, prepare sauce.

Shrimp Sauce: Melt 4 tablespoons of butter in a large sauté pan. Add onions and cook until soft. Stir in shrimp, herbes de Provence, and Cajun seasoning. Add remaining 4 tablespoons of butter and cook, stirring constantly, until sauce thickens.

Cut grits into serving portions and cover with sauce. Garnish with parsley, bacon, and lemon wedges.

—*Dana*, KENTUCKY

Low-Fat Barbecued Shrimp

Makes 4 Servings

Nonfat butter-flavor cooking spray, for frying
2 cloves garlic, chopped
Creole seasoning, to taste
2 tablespoons Worcestershire sauce
1 teaspoon liquid crab boil
2 tablespoons white wine
2 pounds (21–25) large shrimp, unpeeled, without heads
French bread, for serving

Spray a 9-inch skillet with cooking oil. Add garlic, Creole seasoning, Worcestershire sauce, crab boil, and wine. Stir to combine and cook until heated through. Add the unpeeled shrimp. Stir constantly and cook for 3 minutes or until the shrimp are pink and opaque. Serve with French bread.

—*Thomas,* LOUISIANA

Stir-Fried Shrimp

Makes 4 Servings

1 tablespoon cornstarch

⅓ cup dry sherry

3 tablespoons peanut oil, divided

1 pound raw shrimp, peeled

1 teaspoon garlic, minced

1 teaspoon ginger, minced

½ cup water chestnuts, sliced

2 cups Chinese cabbage, cut into thin strips

1 cup green pepper, cut into wedges

20 snow pea pods

3 tablespoons soy sauce

½ cup fish or chicken stock

¼ cup scallions, chopped

Salt and pepper to taste

2 cups rice, cooked

In a small bowl, blend cornstarch with sherry and set aside. In a wok or skillet over high heat, sauté shrimp in 2 tablespoons of peanut oil for about 2 minutes. Do not overcook. Remove shrimp and set aside. Add remaining 1 tablespoon of peanut oil to skillet. Add garlic and ginger and sauté for a few seconds. Add water chestnuts, cabbage, green pepper, and pea pods. Cook, stirring continuously. Add soy sauce, stock, scallions, salt, and pepper. Continue to stir and cook until pea pods are heated through, but still firm. Stir cornstarch/sherry mixture into vegetables and cook for 1 minute. Add sautéed shrimp, and cook an additional 2 minutes, stirring until heated. Serve immediately with rice.

—*Robbie,* NORTH CAROLINA

Shrimp Pontchartrain

Makes 4 Servings

1½ pounds shrimp, peeled and deveined
1 teaspoon Creole seasoning
3 tablespoons butter
1 cup green onions, chopped
6 fresh mushrooms, sliced
¼ cup flour
½ cup half & half, warmed
¼ cup vermouth
1 teaspoon salt
¼ teaspoon cayenne pepper
Spinach linguine, cooked

Bring a medium saucepan ⅔ full of water to a boil. Add shrimp and Creole seasoning and simmer, stirring occasionally, until shrimp turn pink and are almost cooked through but still translucent in the center, about 3 minutes. Drain shrimp, reserving ½ cup of stock. Cover shrimp and set aside.

Melt butter in a large saucepan. Add green onions and mushrooms. Sauté until mushrooms are tender. Add flour; stir well. Slowly stir in reserved shrimp stock, half & half, vermouth, salt, and cayenne pepper; blend well. Cook until sauce is thick and smooth, about 10 minutes. Drain shrimp again, add shrimp to the sauce, and cook an additional 2 minutes. Serve hot over spinach linguine, with a side of fresh asparagus or a green salad.

—*Don*, LOUISIANA

Greek-Style Shrimp

Makes 4 Servings

2 tablespoons olive oil
1 cup green onions, sliced
4 large cloves garlic, minced
1 pound large shrimp, shelled and deveined
¾ cup V-8™ juice
⅓ cup feta cheese
2 tablespoons fresh parsley, chopped
Dash pepper, freshly ground
French bread or cooked rice, for serving

In a 10-inch skillet over medium heat, cook onion with garlic in the olive oil. When onion is tender, add shrimp. Cook, stirring constantly, until shrimp are pink and opaque. Stir in V-8™ juice. Bring to a boil. Reduce heat to low and simmer for 2 minutes. Sprinkle with cheese, parsley, and pepper. Serve over slices of French bread or rice.

—*Joan*, SOUTH CAROLINA

Paella Madrid

Makes 4 Servings

½-pound medium shrimp, shell left on,
    butterflied, and rinsed
Salt, to taste
Pepper, coarsely ground, to taste
1 tablespoon extra virgin olive oil
2 large chicken thighs, boned and quartered
2 ounces chorizo sausage, thinly sliced
2 large shallots, chopped
3 medium cloves garlic, chopped
2 ounces string beans, cut in ½-inch lengths
1 cup Spanish short-grain rice
½ cup parsley, very finely minced, divided
2 cups chicken stock
½ teaspoon saffron
1 teaspoon paprika
12 large mussels
1 large red pepper, roasted, peeled, seeded,
    cut into 8 strips

Sprinkle shrimp with salt and pepper. Refrigerate for ½ hour.
Heat the olive oil over medium-high heat in a large wok. Season
the chicken thighs with salt and pepper. Add them to the hot oil
with the skin side down. Cook until the skin begins to brown,
about 2 minutes. Add the sausage slices and toss with the chicken.
Cook for 1 minute. Add the shallots, garlic, and string beans;
mix well. Add the rice and half of the parsley, stirring to coat
the rice thoroughly with the oil. Add the chicken stock, saffron,
and paprika. Stir well. Bring the mixture to a boil, reduce heat
to medium-low, and cover tightly. Simmer, without disturbing,
for 15 minutes. Lift the cover, embed the shrimp around the rice,
scatter the mussels around the shrimp, and arrange the roasted
red pepper over the rice in a decorative pattern. Cover and cook
until almost all the liquid has been absorbed and the rice is just
cooked, about 10 minutes longer. Sprinkle with remaining parsley.
Serve out of the cooking vessel.

—*Jeanette*, SOUTH CAROLINA

New Orleans–Style Jambalaya

Makes 12 Servings

2 tablespoons cooking oil

1 pound ham or smoked sausage, diced

1 large onion, chopped

1 bell pepper, chopped

2 cups celery, chopped

2 cloves garlic, minced

3 cups chicken, diced

4 cups chicken stock

1 (16-ounce) can tomatoes (optional)

1–1½ teaspoons salt

1 teaspoon pepper

2 bay leaves

2 cups long grain rice, uncooked

2 pounds shrimp, peeled and deveined

36 large oysters (optional)

In a large cast-iron pot, heat oil; add ham or sausage, and sauté for 5 minutes. Add onions, bell pepper, celery, and garlic. Sauté until tender but firm. Add chicken and cook for about 20 minutes. Add chicken stock, tomatoes if desired, salt, pepper, and bay leaves; bring to a boil. Add rice and shrimp. Add oysters, if desired. Stir gently to mix ingredients. Cover and cook on low for about 40 minutes. IMPORTANT: Do not stir! Add a small amount of liquid if needed. Check after 30 minutes to determine if rice is cooked through, but firm.

—*Becky,* LOUISIANA

Oyster Rockefeller Casserole

Makes 8 Servings

2½ sticks (1¼ cups) butter
½ teaspoon thyme
½ bunch green onions, finely chopped
¾ cup French breadcrumbs
2–3 dozen shelled oysters, drained
¼ cup parsley, chopped
½ cup water
1½ tablespoons anise seed
2 pounds spinach, chopped
Salt and pepper, to taste

Preheat oven to 425°F. Melt butter in a large skillet. Add thyme and green onions and sauté for about 2 minutes. Add breadcrumbs and sauté until breadcrumbs are golden brown. Reduce heat and add drained oysters. Simmer until oysters curl up on the edges. Toss with the parsley and set aside. In a medium pot, combine the water and anise seed and bring to a boil. Boil for 10 minutes. While water is boiling, set spinach over the pot in a stainless steel or bamboo steamer. Don't be afraid to compress the spinach a bit to get it to fit into the steamer. Steam the spinach until it is just barely wilted, about 2 minutes. Stir spinach into oyster mixture. Strain the anise from the water. Add water to oyster mixture. Mix well. Season to taste with salt and pepper. Pour into a 2-quart casserole dish. Bake 20–25 minutes.

—*Donna*, LOUISIANA

Oyster Soufflé

Makes 4 Servings

2 tablespoons margarine
1 cup celery, finely chopped
1 cup cracker crumbs, divided
2 cups oysters
Salt, to taste
Pepper, to taste
1 (13¾-ounce) can chicken broth
2 eggs, beaten

Melt margarine in a medium skillet. Add celery and sauté until softened. Set aside. Spread ¼ cup of the cracker crumbs in the bottom of a 2-quart casserole. Spread 1 cup of the oysters on top of crumbs. Spread celery on top of oysters. Season with salt and pepper. Cover with remaining the oysters. Sprinkle ½ cup of the cracker crumbs over the oysters. Pour the chicken broth over the top of the casserole; let stand 30 minutes.

Preheat oven to 350°F. Bake for 10 minutes. Remove from oven. Pour beaten eggs on top of the casserole and cover with remaining ¼ cup of cracker crumbs. Return to the oven and bake for an additional 15–20 minutes or until eggs are set, but not hard.

—*Vernell*, GEORGIA

The Oyster—the mere writing of the word
creates sensations of succulence—
gastronomical pleasures, nutritive fare,
easy digestion, palatable indulgence—
then go to sleep in peace.

—LUCULLUS

Fried Frog Legs

Makes 4 Servings

2 pounds frog legs
Salt, to taste
Pepper, to taste
Juice from ½ lemon
2 eggs, well beaten
2 cups fine dry breadcrumbs
Cooking oil, for frying

In a large pot, add water and bring to a boil. Skin frog legs and cut off feet. Remove tendons, or while the legs are frying, they will jump out of the pan. Salt boiling water and season it with pepper and lemon juice. Scald frog legs in the water, cooking for about 4 minutes. Drain legs and pat dry. Dip legs into eggs and then roll in breadcrumbs. Heat oil in a deep-fat fryer or deep skillet to 375°F. Fry for 3 minutes or until legs are tender.

—*Jerry*, ARKANSAS

Spinach Sauce with Ricotta and Bacon over Pasta

Makes 6 Servings

12 ounces bacon, cooked and crumbled,
   drippings reserved
¼ pound butter, divided
2 pounds fresh spinach, rinsed, lightly steamed,
   squeezed dry, and chopped
Salt, to taste
⅛ teaspoon nutmeg, freshly grated
1 pound rigatoni, cooked and drained
½ cup fresh ricotta cheese
½ cup Parmesan cheese, freshly grated,
   plus more for serving

Heat the reserved bacon drippings and half of the butter in a large pan. Add spinach and sauté while seasoning with liberal pinches of salt, for about 2 minutes. Stir frequently. Add cooked, crumbled bacon and mix well. Remove from heat and stir in the grated nutmeg. Add the pasta, ricotta, and Parmesan, and toss well. Serve immediately with grated Parmesan on the side.

—*Dr. Tim,* SOUTH CAROLINA

Fried Ham
and Red Eye Gravy

Makes 4 Servings

1 pound ham, sliced
1 cup strong black coffee
Grease, for frying

Melt a small amount of grease in an iron skillet over medium heat.
Place sliced ham in the skillet and cook until browned on both sides.
Remove ham from skillet. Leave several tablespoons of grease
and ham residue in the skillet. Drain and discard excess grease.
Pour coffee into skillet and stir over medium heat for 5 minutes.
You've got yourself red eye gravy. Serve with biscuits and grits.

—*Sally*, GEORGIA

Baked Ham
with Burgundy Glaze

Makes 8 to 12 Servings

1 (10–15 pound) ham, drained, with rind
    and all but ¼-inch of fat removed
Whole cloves (optional)
½ cup brown sugar, firmly packed
1 (6-ounce) can orange juice concentrate, thawed
1 cup Burgundy
½ teaspoon cinnamon
½ teaspoon dry mustard

Preheat oven to 350°F. Score ham in a diamond pattern. If desired,
center each diamond with a clove. Place ham in a deep baking pan.
In a saucepan, combine brown sugar, orange juice, Burgundy,
cinnamon, and mustard. Simmer for 5 minutes, stirring constantly.
Pour glaze over ham. Bake for about an hour and 15 minutes,
basting every 15 minutes, until ham is heated through. Skim fat
off of remaining sauce and serve in a gravy boat.

—*Trinity United Methodist Church*, VIRGINIA

Sausage Roll Ring

Makes 2 to 3 Servings

2 cups flour
Pinch of salt
½ cup butter
½ cup water (or as needed)
½ pound ground sausage, cooked and crumbled
1 cup onion, chopped
1 egg, beaten

Preheat oven to 425°F. Sift flour and salt into a medium bowl. Cut butter into flour until mixture resembles coarse crumbs. Gradually add water to make a slightly sticky dough. On a floured surface, roll the dough into an 18x4-inch rectangle. Spread cooked and crumbled sausage over pastry, leaving a ¾-inch space around the edges of the dough. Sprinkle the chopped onion over the sausage. Dampen one long side of pastry with water. Starting with the opposite long side, roll the dough into a tube shape and place seamed side down. Shape the roll into a ring and seal the ends to create a circle. Brush pastry with beaten egg. Place the sausage ring in a lightly oiled baking pan. Bake for 20–25 minutes or until pastry is golden brown.

—*Bobbie,* NORTH CAROLINA

Boudin

Makes 75 3-Inch Sausages

2 pounds pork
3 pounds pork liver
1 pound pork heart
2 large onions
1 bell pepper
2 cloves garlic
1 quart water
5–6 cups rice, cooked
1 bunch green onions, minced
25 feet casings

Using a meat grinder, combine pork, liver, heart, onions, bell pepper, and garlic. Pour into a large pot. Add water, and simmer until meat is tender. Stir in cooked rice and green onions. Tie one end of casings. Use a sausage stuffer to fill casings with the pork stuffing. Tie open end of casings. Cook finished sausages in hot (not boiling) water for about 30 minutes. Serve.

—*Jean*, LOUISIANA

Joe's Red Beans

Makes 6 to 8 Servings

2 pounds red kidney beans
2 large onions, chopped
2 large bell peppers, chopped
1 clove garlic, minced
2 bay leaves
2 cups of Claret wine (or your favorite)
5 cups of water, divided
   (divided into 3 cups and then 2)
5 sausage links, cut into 1-inch pieces
2 cups of ham, cooked and chopped
Salt and pepper, to taste
3–4 cups of cooked rice, for serving

In large bowl, add all ingredients except the meat; stir to mix. Add 3 cups of water and refrigerate overnight.

Remove from refrigerator and add 2 more cups of water. Pour into large saucepan and bring to a boil. Simmer for 2 hours. Add the sausage and ham. Simmer for 30 minutes. Salt and pepper to taste. Serve over rice.

—*Bettye and Joe*, MISSISSIPPI

Favorite Red Beans and Rice

Makes 8 Servings

1 pound dried red beans
1¾ quarts water
1 pound smoked sausage, sliced
2 large Bermuda onions, chopped
1 bunch green onions, chopped
1 cup parsley, chopped
1 teaspoon garlic, minced
1 tablespoon salt
¼ teaspoon cayenne pepper
1 teaspoon black pepper
½ teaspoon sugar
¼ teaspoon Tabasco™ sauce
¼ teaspoon oregano
¼ teaspoon thyme
1 tablespoon Worcestershire sauce
1 (8-ounce) can tomato sauce
1 teaspoon seasoned salt
8 cups rice, cooked, for serving

Wash beans well and place in a large bowl; cover with water and soak overnight. Drain. In a large Dutch oven, combine soaked and drained beans, sausage, Bermuda onions, green onions, parsley, garlic, salt, cayenne pepper, black pepper, sugar, Tabasco,™ oregano, thyme, Worcestershire sauce, and tomato sauce. Bring to a boil. Reduce heat and cook slowly for 3½ hours, stirring occasionally. Add seasoned salt and cook for an additional 30 minutes. Remove 2 cups of mixture from the pot and transfer to a bowl. Mash well, almost to a creamy consistency. Return to pot and stir. Serve over rice.

—*Margaret*, MISSISSIPPI

German Potatoes and Sausage

Makes 6 Servings

3 tablespoons oil
2½ pounds small red potatoes,
    cut in ¼-inch slices
2 medium onions, cut into small wedges
½ head green cabbage, cut into 1-inch pieces
1 (16-ounce) package smoked sausages,
    cut into ¼-inch slices
Salt, to taste
Pepper, to taste

Heat oil in a large skillet. Add potatoes; fry for 5 minutes, turning occasionally. Add onions. Fry until potatoes are light brown, continuing to turn occasionally. Add cabbage and cook until all vegetables are tender. Add sausage. Salt and pepper to taste. Cook until sausage is heated through, about 5 minutes.

—*Jeanette*, NORTH CAROLINA

Pray for peace and grace and spiritual food,
For wisdom and guidance, for all these are good,
But don't forget the potatoes.

—JOHN TYLER PETTEE

Ribs and Sauerkraut

Makes 6 Servings

4 pounds pork ribs
Salt, to taste
Pepper, to taste
1 quart (4 cups) sauerkraut
1 apple, cored and quartered
2 tablespoons brown sugar
1 tablespoon caraway seeds
1 onion, sliced
2 cups water

Season meat with salt and pepper and brown in a large skillet. In a crock-pot, combine sauerkraut, apple, sugar, caraway seeds, and onion. Place browned ribs on top of the sauerkraut mixture. Pour water into the crock-pot and cover tightly. Simmer until meat is very tender, about 1½ hours.

—*Nancy,* TENNESSEE

Baked Barbequed Spare Ribs

Makes 6 Servings

4 pounds country-style pork spareribs
1 medium onion, finely chopped
2 tablespoons butter
2 tablespoons cider vinegar
2 tablespoons vegetable oil
2 tablespoons Worcestershire sauce
$\frac{1}{8}$ teaspoon cayenne pepper
½ tablespoon ground mustard
½ teaspoon pepper
1 teaspoon salt
¼ cup brown sugar, packed
¼ cup lemon juice
1 cup ketchup
1 cup water
½ teaspoon garlic, minced

Preheat oven to 350°F. In a medium bowl, add all ingredients except ribs; stir to blend. Place ribs in a 10x15-inch baking dish. Pour sauce over ribs and bake uncovered until meat starts to pull away from the bone, 1½–2 hours. These ribs can be prepared up to a day in advance and allowed to marinate.

—*Stephanie*, TENNESSEE

Maple Country Ribs

Makes 4 Servings

3 pounds country-style pork ribs
1 cup pure maple syrup
½ cup applesauce
¼ cup ketchup
3 tablespoons lemon juice
¼ teaspoon salt
¼ teaspoon pepper
¼ teaspoon paprika
¼ teaspoon garlic powder
¼ teaspoon ground cinnamon

Preheat oven to 325°F. Place ribs in a large pot, cover with water and boil until tender. Transfer ribs to a greased baking pan. In a small bowl, combine syrup, applesauce, ketchup, lemon juice, salt, pepper, paprika, garlic powder, and cinnamon. Mix well. Pour half of the sauce over the ribs. Bake uncovered for 20–30 minutes, basting often with the remaining sauce.

—*Shirley,* MISSISSIPPI

Bary's Favorite Pork Chops

Makes 4 Servings

4 pork chops, medium thickness
2 tablespoons vegetable oil
1 clove garlic, minced
¾ cup sherry
¼ cup soy sauce
¼ cup vegetable oil
1 tablespoon ginger, minced
¼ teaspoon oregano
1 tablespoon maple syrup

Preheat oven to 350°F. In a large skillet, brown chops in vegetable oil. Place browned chops in a large baking dish. Combine remaining ingredients in a medium bowl. Pour over chops. Bake uncovered for 1 hour, turning once.

—*Tina,* SOUTH CAROLINA

Coca-Cola™ Chops

Makes 8 Servings

8 pork chops
Salt, to taste
Pepper, to taste
1 cup ketchup
2 tablespoons Worcestershire sauce
1 cup Coca-Cola™
Brown sugar, to taste

Preheat oven to 350°F. Place chops in a large baking dish. Season with salt and pepper. Mix ketchup, Worcestershire sauce, and Coca-Cola™ in a small bowl; pour over chops. Sprinkle with brown sugar. Bake uncovered for 1 hour. You can use chicken breasts instead of pork chops, if you'd like.

—*Yvonne and Judy,* SOUTH CAROLINA

Pork Chops and Apples

Makes 6 Servings

6 pork chops
4 Granny Smith apples, sliced
½ teaspoon cinnamon
¼ cup brown sugar
2 tablespoons butter

Preheat oven to 400°F. Spray skillet with non-stick cooking spray. Add pork chops and cook until browned. Place apples in a greased 13x9-inch baking dish. Sprinkle with cinnamon and brown sugar. Dot with butter. Arrange browned chops over apples. Cover with foil and bake for 1½ hours.

—*Joy,* TENNESSEE

Caramel Apple Pork Chops

Makes 4 Servings

4 boneless pork chops, ¾-inch thick
Vegetable oil, for frying
2 tablespoons brown sugar
Salt and pepper, to taste
⅛ teaspoon ground mace
⅛ teaspoon ground nutmeg
2 tablespoons butter
2 Granny Smith apples, peeled, cored,
    and cut into ½-inch wedges
3 tablespoons pecans, chopped

Brush chops lightly with oil and cook over medium-high heat for about 10 minutes, turning occasionally. Cook until evenly browned and juices run clear when chops are pierced with a fork. Remove chops from skillet and keep warm.

In a small bowl, combine brown sugar, salt, pepper, mace, and nutmeg. Melt butter in skillet; stir in brown sugar mixture and apples. Cover and cook 8–10 minutes until apples are tender. Remove apples with a slotted spoon and arrange on top of chops. Keep warm.

Continue cooking the mixture in skillet, uncovered, until sauce thickens slightly. Spoon sauce over apples and pork chops. Sprinkle with pecans and serve.

—*Vicki*, MISSISSIPPI

Vincent's Fruity Pork Loin

Makes 6 Servings

MARINADE:

½ cup vinegar
½ cup Italian dressing
¼ cup olive oil
1 tablespoon fresh ginger, grated
2 tablespoons white wine

¼ cup raisins
¾ cup dried figs, chopped
2 tablespoons apricot-pineapple preserves
2 tablespoons pecans, minced

PORK:

4–5 pounds pork loin roast
4 cloves garlic, thickly sliced
Salt, to taste
Pepper, to taste
1 tablespoon flour

1 medium onion, sliced
Small bunch rosemary, if desired
2 tablespoons wine
½ cup water

Marinade: In a medium saucepan, add all marinade ingredients and stir to combine. Simmer for 20 minutes. Set aside.

Pork: In a small bowl, toss the garlic with salt and pepper. Slit holes in roast and stuff with seasonings. Place roast in a plastic freezer bag; add marinade. Refrigerate 6–8 hours or overnight.

Preheat oven to 325°F. Place the flour in an oven bag and shake it thoroughly to coat sides of bag. Make a bed of onions and rosemary on the bottom of the bag; set aside. Drain roast, reserving marinade. Dab excess moisture from the roast with a paper towel. Season roast with salt and pepper. Place seasoned roast in the oven bag containing flour, onions, and rosemary. Add wine and water to the oven bag. Bake 2–2¼ hours, until center of pork registers 160°F on a meat thermometer.

In a saucepan, heat marinade to slightly reduce liquid. Serve marinade with the roast.

—*Clair*, LOUISIANA

Grilled Spiced Rubbed Pork Tenderloin

Makes 2 to 3 Servings

3 tablespoons cooking oil
¼ teaspoon cayenne pepper
1 teaspoon dried thyme
⅛ teaspoon nutmeg
1 tablespoon brown sugar
½ teaspoon wine vinegar
¾ teaspoon salt
¼ teaspoon black pepper
1–1½ pounds pork tenderloin

Prepare barbeque grill for direct cooking over medium heat. In a small bowl, combine all ingredients except the pork tenderloin. Pierce pork with a fork and rub the seasoning mixture onto the meat. Let stand for several minutes to allow pork to absorb flavors of the mixture. Grill 15–30 minutes, turning once. When a thermometer inserted in the center of the tenderloin registers 140°F, remove from heat, and cover with foil. Let stand for 10 minutes before serving.

—*Penny,* NORTH CAROLINA

Nanny's Southern Fried Chicken

Makes 4 Servings

2 eggs
2 tablespoons water
3 cups flour, divided equally into 2 pie pans
Garlic salt, for seasoning
Paprika, for seasoning
1 (4-pound) fryer chicken, cut into pieces
Salt and pepper, for seasoning
Vegetable oil, for frying

In a medium bowl, beat eggs with water. Season one pan of flour with garlic salt and paprika. Season chicken with salt and pepper. Dip chicken in plain flour, dip in egg wash, and then dip in seasoned flour. Heat oil in a deep frying pan. Place coated chicken pieces in heated oil. Cook for approximately 15 minutes, turning frequently, until all sides are browned. Reduce heat to medium-low and cook uncovered, for an additional 30–45 minutes, turning often. Chicken is cooked through when it is no longer pink inside. Drain on paper towels.

—*Sally*, SOUTH CAROLINA

" *To know about fried chicken you have to have been weaned and reared in the South. Period.* "

—JAMES VILLAS

Deep-Fried Chicken Livers

Makes 4 Servings

1½ cups buttermilk
1 pound chicken livers, excess fat removed
Vegetable oil, for frying
1 cup flour
2 teaspoons Old Bay™ Seasoning
1 teaspoon salt
½ teaspoon black pepper
¼ teaspoon red pepper

Pour buttermilk into a re-sealable bag; add chicken livers. Seal bag and shake well. Refrigerate bag containing buttermilk and chicken livers for at least 2 hours.

In a deep fryer, preheat vegetable oil to 325°F. In a medium bowl, mix flour, Old Bay™ Seasoning, salt, and peppers. Drain excess buttermilk from the livers, and lightly dredge livers in the flour mixture. Carefully place livers, one at a time, in the hot vegetable oil. Fry 3–5 minutes, or until cooked through. Livers may float to the top of the oil when they are nearly cooked. The center of the livers will no longer be pink or red, if thoroughly cooked. Drain on paper towels. Serve immediately.

—*Reverend & Mrs.,* GEORGIA

Lemon Barbequed Chicken

Makes 8 Servings

1–2 small broiler chickens
¾ cup vegetable oil
¾ cup fresh lemon juice
1 tablespoon salt
¼ cup vinegar
1 teaspoon paprika
2 teaspoons basil, crushed
2 teaspoons onion powder
½ teaspoon thyme, crushed
½ teaspoon garlic powder

Cut chicken into halves or quarters and place in a shallow baking pan. Combine all other ingredients in a jar and shake well to blend. Pour sauce over the chicken, cover tightly, and marinate in the refrigerator 6–8 hours or overnight, turning chicken occasionally. Remove chicken about an hour before grilling, reserving sauce.

Spray the grill rack with nonstick cooking spray and prepare grill for cooking over medium heat. Place chicken, skin side up, on the grill and cook for 20–25 minutes, brushing often with the reserved sauce. Turn chicken and cook for an additional 20 minutes.

Chicken may be baked in the oven. Transfer chicken to a broiler pan, place pan 8 inches from the broiler, set oven to broil, and brush chicken often with sauce. Cooking time will be less than when grilling the chicken.

—*Ann and James,* MISSISSIPPI

Chicken Kabobs Supreme

Makes 4 Servings

2 whole chicken breasts, skinned, boned,
   and cut into 1-inch cubes
½ cup vegetable oil
¼ cup soy sauce
¼ cup dry white wine
½ cup light corn syrup
1 tablespoon sesame seeds
2 tablespoons lemon juice
¼ teaspoon garlic powder
¼ teaspoon ground ginger
1 small pineapple, cubed
1 large green bell pepper, cut into 1-inch pieces
2 medium onions, quartered
3 small zucchini, cut into 1-inch cubes
½ pound fresh mushroom caps
1 pint cherry tomatoes

In a large bowl, combine the vegetable oil, soy sauce, wine, corn syrup, sesame seeds, lemon juice, garlic powder, and ginger. Mix well. Stir in the chicken. Cover and refrigerate at least 2 hours.

Prepare grill for cooking over medium-hot coals. Remove chicken from marinade, reserving marinade. Prepare skewers with alternating pieces of chicken, pineapple, pepper, onions, zucchini, mushroom caps, and tomatoes. Grill, basting often with the marinade, until vegetables are soft and chicken is thoroughly cooked, about 15–20 minutes.

—*Kellyanne*, SOUTH CAROLINA

Oven-Barbequed Wrapped Chicken Breasts

Makes 6 Servings

⅓ cup red onion, minced
1 teaspoon garlic, minced
½ cup ketchup
¼ cup lemon juice
1 teaspoon basil
¼ cup olive oil
1 tablespoon honey
1 tablespoon Worcestershire sauce
1 tablespoon cream-style horseradish
2 teaspoons Creole seasoning
6 boneless chicken breasts
Salt, to taste
Pepper, to taste
12 slices bacon

Preheat oven to 375°F. In a medium saucepan, mix the first 10 ingredients. Cook over low heat, stirring until well blended, about 5 minutes.

Salt and pepper the chicken. Wrap 2 slices of bacon, one at a time, around each chicken breast. Secure with a toothpick. Brush breasts with the sauce and place in a shallow baking pan. Bake for 45 minutes. Turn and baste with sauce every 10 minutes during baking.

—*Marie*, MISSISSIPPI

Lime-Sauced Chicken

Makes 4 Servings

4 chicken breasts, skinless and boneless
Juice of 1 lime
¾ cup apple juice
2 teaspoons cornstarch
1 chicken flavor bullion cube

Preheat oven to warm. Spray a skillet with nonstick cooking spray. Preheat skillet over medium heat. Add the chicken breasts. Cook 8–10 minutes, turning breasts to assure even browning, until cooked through. Transfer chicken from the skillet to an ovenproof dish and place in the warm oven.

In a small bowl, combine lime juice, apple juice, cornstarch, and bouillon cube. Pour mixture into skillet and cook, stirring until thick. Spoon sauce over chicken and serve.

—*Avis,* MISSISSIPPI

Chicken Breasts with Orange Sauce

Makes 6 Servings

6 chicken breasts
1/3 cup sugar
2 tablespoons flour
2 cups fresh-squeezed orange juice
Zest of 1 orange
2 tablespoons lemon juice
Salt, to taste
Pepper, to taste

Preheat oven to 350°F. Brown chicken in a large oven-proof skillet. Cover skillet and bake in the oven for 40 minutes.

Combine sugar and flour in the top of a double boiler. Gradually stir in the orange juice. Add the orange zest and lemon juice. Season with salt and pepper. Cook until sauce thickens and the flour looses its raw taste.

Pour sauce over chicken and bake an additional 10 minutes, basting chicken frequently with sauce.

—*Leilah,* TENNESSEE

Chicken and Dumplings

This dish was a basic at all family gatherings, holidays, and church suppers. It is a dish made by the grandmothers and served over rice.

Makes 4 Servings

1 tablespoon salt

$6^2/_3$ cups water, divided

1 whole chicken

2 cups flour

1 teaspoon baking powder

4 tablespoons shortening

1 tablespoon butter

Black pepper, to taste

Cooked rice, for serving

In a large pot, add salt to 6 cups of water; bring to a boil. Add chicken and boil until tender and cooked through. Remove chicken leaving the broth in the pot over low heat. Skin, debone, and cut chicken into small pieces. Set aside. Sift flour and baking powder into a large bowl. Using 2 butter knives, cut in shortening until dough is crumbly. Add ⅔ cup water and stir until just combined. Dough will be stiff. Roll out on a lightly floured surface until thin. Cut into 2-inch squares. Bring chicken broth back to a boil. Drop dough squares into boiling broth. Add butter and pepper to the broth. Reduce heat to medium-low and simmer, uncovered, for about 20 minutes, or until dumplings are cooked. Return chicken to pot to warm before serving. Serve over rice.

—*Emily & Kathleen*, LOUISIANA

Chicken Cakes with Creole Sauce

Makes 4 Servings

2 tablespoons butter

1 small red bell pepper, diced

4 green onions, thinly sliced

1 clove garlic, pressed

1 large egg, lightly beaten

2 tablespoons mayonnaise

1 tablespoon Creole mustard

2 teaspoons Creole seasoning

3 cups chicken, cooked and chopped

1 cup soft breadcrumbs

¼ cup vegetable oil

Chopped fresh parsley, for garnish

Creole sauce, for serving

Melt butter in a large non-stick skillet. Add bell pepper, green onions, and garlic and sauté until tender, about 3–4 minutes. In a large bowl, add lightly beaten egg, mayonnaise, Creole mustard, and Creole seasoning; stir to combine. Transfer sautéed vegetables into the bowl with the egg mixture and add chicken and breadcrumbs; stir until thoroughly mixed. Shape mixture into 8 (3½-inch) patties. Heat 2 tablespoons vegetable oil in a large skillet. Carefully place the patties in the pan. Fry them for about 3 minutes per side, or until golden brown. Drain on paper towels. Add 2 more tablespoons of oil to the pan, and repeat procedure with remaining patties. Garnish with chopped parsley, and serve immediately with Creole sauce.

—*Delores*, ARKANSAS

Chicken Pie
with Sweet Potato Crust

Makes 8 Servings

CHICKEN FILLING:
3 cups chicken, cooked and diced
1 cup carrots, cooked and sliced
6 small white onions, quartered and sautéed
1 tablespoon parsley, chopped
3 tablespoons flour
1 cup milk
1 cup chicken broth
Salt and pepper, for seasoning

SWEET POTATO CRUST:
2 cups flour
1 teaspoon baking powder
½ teaspoon salt
$\frac{1}{3}$ cup shortening
1 cup sweet potatoes, cooked, mashed, and chilled
1 egg, beaten

Chicken Filling: Layer cooked chicken, carrots, sautéed onions, and parsley in a greased 2½-quart casserole. Set aside. In a large saucepan, combine flour and a small amount of milk, blending until smooth. Gradually stir in remaining milk and chicken broth. Cook over low heat until thickened. Add salt and pepper, to taste. Pour milk/chicken broth sauce over the chicken and vegetables. Prepare sweet potato crust.

Sweet Potato Crust: Preheat oven to 350°F. In a large mixing bowl, combine flour, baking powder, and salt. Using 2 butter knives, cut in shortening until mixture resembles coarse crumbs. Do not over-mix. Add cooked, mashed sweet potatoes and beaten egg; mix. Roll out dough on a lightly floured surface to ¼-inch thickness. Cover the casserole with sweet potato crust and bake for 45 minutes.

—*Irma,* GEORGIA

Spoonbread Chicken Pie

Makes 6 Servings

CHICKEN FILLING:
6 tablespoons butter
¼ cup celery, chopped
6 tablespoons flour
2½ cups chicken broth
1 teaspoon onion salt
½ teaspoon salt
½ teaspoon pepper
1 tablespoon dried parsley
3 cups chicken, cooked and chopped

SPOONBREAD:
3 eggs
1 cup self-rising cornmeal
2 cups boiling water
1 cup buttermilk

Chicken Filling: Preheat oven to 400°F. In large heated skillet, melt butter and sauté celery. Add flour and stir well. Add chicken broth. Stir and cook until thickened. Add onion salt, salt, pepper, and parsley. Stir in the cooked, chopped chicken. Pour into a 9x13-inch baking pan and bake for 10 minutes. Remove from oven.

Spoonbread: In a large mixing bowl, beat eggs; add cornmeal, boiling water, and buttermilk. Stir well. Pour on top of hot chicken.

Return baking dish to oven. Bake for an additional 30–40 minutes or until browned.

—*Wilma,* MISSISSIPPI

Angel Hair Pasta with Lemon and Chicken

Makes 4 Servings

1 (9-ounce) package angel hair pasta
1½ cups chicken, cooked and diced
⅓ cup butter, melted
2 tablespoons lemon juice
2 tablespoons fresh parsley, chopped
¼ teaspoon marjoram
¼ teaspoon garlic powder
Salt, to taste
Pepper, to taste

Prepare pasta according to package directions. Add the remaining ingredients to the drained pasta. Simmer and stir until heated through. Salt and pepper to taste.

—*Avis*, MISSISSIPPI

You don't have to cook fancy or complicated masterpieces— just good food from fresh ingredients.

—JULIA CHILD

Greek Feta Chicken

Makes 4 Servings

8 ounces low fat yogurt
1 tablespoon lemon juice
½ teaspoon dried oregano
½ teaspoon dried rosemary
¼ teaspoon pepper
1 large clove garlic, chopped
4 (4-ounce) chicken breasts, skinned and boned
¼ cup feta cheese, crumbled
1 tablespoon fresh parsley

In a large heavy-duty zip-top plastic bag, combine yogurt, lemon juice, oregano, rosemary, pepper, and garlic; stir to blend. Add chicken, seal the bag, and shake until chicken is well coated. Marinate in the refrigerator for 30 minutes.

Remove chicken from the bag and reserve marinade. Coat broiler pan with nonstick cooking spray and place chicken on the broiler pan. Set oven temperature to broil. Carefully place broiler pan with chicken 5½ inches from heat source and broil for 7 minutes. Turn chicken over, broil an additional 7 minutes or until chicken is cooked through. Spoon reserved marinade over chicken and top with feta cheese. Return to broiler for 2 minutes or until marinade is warm and cheese is melted. Sprinkle with parsley and serve.

—*Ina*, NORTH CAROLINA

Stir-Fried Chinese Chicken with Cashews

Makes 4 Servings

1 egg white, lightly beaten
½ cup soy sauce, divided
1 tablespoon plus 1 teaspoon cornstarch
1½ pound boneless chicken breasts, cut into 1-inch cubes
1 tablespoon dry sherry
2 teaspoons cider vinegar
1 teaspoon sugar
¼ cup vegetable oil
⅔ cup unsalted cashews
¼ teaspoon ground ginger
2 green onions, chopped
1 (8-ounce) can sliced water chestnuts, drained
1 medium green bell pepper, coarsely diced
Cooked white rice, for serving

In a medium bowl, combine lightly beaten egg, 1 tablespoon of soy sauce, and 1 tablespoon cornstarch. Add chicken cubes and toss to coat. Let stand 15 minutes.

In a small bowl, combine remaining soy sauce, 1 teaspoon of cornstarch, sherry, vinegar, and sugar; set aside.

In a large frying pan or wok, heat oil over medium-high heat. Add cashews and stir-fry for 1 minute; remove cashews with slotted spoon and drain on paper towels. Add chicken and stir-fry until opaque, 2–3 minutes. Remove chicken and set aside.

Discard all but about 2 tablespoons oil from the pan or wok. Add ginger, green onions, and water chestnuts; stir-fry 1 minute. Add chicken, bell pepper, and bowl of seasoning sauce. Cook, stirring constantly, until thickened. Add cashews. Serve hot over rice.

—*Stephanie*, TENNESSEE

Chicken and Wild Rice with Dried Cherries

Makes 8 Servings

1½ cups wild rice, rinsed and drained
4 cups water
5 tablespoons unsalted butter, divided
¼ cup plus 1 tablespoon flour
3½ cups chicken broth
2 tablespoons shallots, minced
4 cups mushrooms, sliced
1½ cups heavy cream
$^1/_8$ teaspoon nutmeg, freshly grated
2 tablespoons fresh lemon juice
3 cups chicken, cooked and cubed
1 cup dried cherries plus more for garnish
2 teaspoons salt
Pepper, to taste
Sour cream, for garnish

Combine rice and water in a medium saucepan. Bring to a boil over medium-high heat. Reduce heat to medium-low and simmer, covered, until just tender, 45 minutes to 1 hour.

In a large saucepan, use 4 tablespoons butter and flour to make a light roux. See recipe on page 170. Add the chicken broth to the roux and bring mixture to a boil over high heat. Reduce to medium and simmer, whisking occasionally, for 15 minutes.

Preheat oven to 400°F. While sauce is simmering, cook the shallots and mushrooms in the remaining butter in a large skillet over medium heat, stirring occasionally, until most of the liquid has evaporated. Add the mushroom mixture to the sauce and stir in the cream, nutmeg, lemon juice, chicken, cherries, rice, salt, and pepper. Transfer mixture to a 13x9-inch baking dish and bake covered in the middle of oven for 20 minutes. Uncover and continue to bake until most of the liquid has been reabsorbed, 15–25 minutes longer. Serve hot, garnished with additional cherries and sour cream.

—*Margaret,* SOUTH CAROLINA

Roast Goose
with Orange Stuffing

Makes 6 to 8 Servings

2 tablespoons butter
½ cup onion, chopped
½ cup celery, chopped
8 cups fresh bread cubes, dried slightly
1 cup fresh orange juice
2 tablespoons orange zest
Pepper, freshly ground, to taste
1 cup fresh parsley, chopped
½ teaspoon thyme
½ teaspoon ground sage
2 teaspoons salt
1 (13-pound) goose, rinsed, dried, large fat layers
    and stray pin feathers removed

Preheat oven to 325°F. In a medium skillet, melt butter and sauté
the onions and celery until soft. In a large bowl, mix sautéed onions
and celery with bread cubes. Add all remaining ingredients, except
for goose, and toss gently.

Use a skewer to fasten the neck skin of the goose to its back. Spoon
stuffing into cavity, packing lightly. Truss and place on rack in a
shallow roasting pan. Roast until drumstick meat feels soft to the
touch and joints move easily, about 3½ hours. As the goose roasts,
spoon off any fat that accumulates. Don't do anything else to the
bird. Don't prick it, don't jab it, and don't baste it. But, don't forget
it. Overcooking is the only way you can hurt it.

—*Sally*, SOUTH CAROLINA

Wild Duck with Apple Stuffing

Makes 6 Servings

APPLE STUFFING:
3 tablespoons butter, melted
1 teaspoon salt
1 onion, finely chopped
2 apples, peeled and thinly sliced
½ cup raisins (optional)
3 cups stale cornbread

DUCKS:
2 Mallard or Canvasback ducks (5-6 pounds)
Salt and pepper, for seasoning
3 apples, unpeeled and thinly sliced
4 strips bacon
1½ cups water

Apple Stuffing: In a large bowl, combine melted butter and salt. Add the onion, apples, and raisins (optional) to the butter/salt mixture. Stir in the stale cornbread.

Ducks: Preheat oven to 350°F. Season ducks, inside and out, with salt and pepper. Stuff the ducks with the apple stuffing. Place the ducks in the center of a 15x11-inch baking pan. Arrange the sliced apples and any leftover stuffing around the ducks. Lay two strips of bacon over each duck. Carefully and evenly pour 1½ cups water into the pan. Roast until ducks are tender and cooked through. Add more water if ducks and stuffing begin to dry out.

—*Dolores,* ARKANSAS

Cajun Deep-Fried Turkey

Makes 14 Servings

Before starting this recipe, you'll need a 60-quart boiling pot with basket and elevated outdoor propane burner, a seasoning injector, and a meat thermometer. Don't try to fry a bird that weighs over 14 pounds—it'll take too long to cook, resulting in burnt skin.

4–6 gallons peanut oil
14-pound turkey, thawed
2 sticks (1 cup) butter
1 teaspoon Worcestershire sauce
1 teaspoon Louisiana hot sauce
½ teaspoon onion juice
½ teaspoon garlic juice
6 tablespoons zesty Italian dressing
⅓ cup white wine
1 teaspoon cayenne pepper
1 teaspoon cracked red pepper
1 teaspoon Cajun seasoning

Pour peanut oil into a 60-quart boiling pot and preheat to 375°F over outdoor propane burner. It should take 45–60 minutes for the oil to heat. DO NOT fry your turkey indoors or under a carport. Thoroughly rinse turkey. Drain. Cover, and set aside. In a microwave-safe bowl, mix butter, Worcestershire sauce, Louisiana Hot Sauce, onion juice, garlic juice, zesty Italian dressing, and white wine. Microwave 30–60 seconds on medium power until butter is liquefied. Cool. Once the sauce has cooled, use the seasoning injector to infuse the turkey with the sauce. When you have injected the entire turkey, dust it with the cayenne pepper, cracked red pepper, and Cajun seasoning. Cover the seasoned turkey with wax paper until you are ready to cook the bird. When ready to cook, remove the wax paper. Place the turkey in the frying basket. Wearing heavy-duty leather gloves, lower it SLOWLY into the oil using EXTREME CAUTION. Fry the turkey for about 3½ minutes per pound, 49 minutes for a 14-pound turkey. Turkey

(continued on next page)

may float to the surface of the oil when completely cooked. To test for doneness, carefully remove the turkey from the oil and insert the meat thermometer into its breast. If it measures between 170°F an 180°F, it's done! Let the turkey cool for 20 minutes or more before slicing. Refrigerate any leftover meat within 2 hours of cooking.

—*Delores*, ARKANSAS

Squirrel

Makes 2 Servings

3 squirrels (1 pound), cleaned and deboned
Salt, pepper, or Tony Chachere's™ Original Creole
    Seasoning, to taste
Cooking oil, for frying plus 2 tablespoons, for roux
3 onions
1 cup celery, chopped
2 tablespoons flour
1 cup bell pepper, chopped
2 teaspoons garlic, minced
1 bunch green onions, chopped
3 tablespoons parsley, chopped
Cooked rice, for serving

Cut squirrel meat into bite-sized chunks. Season to taste. Heat oil in a large pot. Cook the meat until browned on all sides. Remove from pot. Using the same pot and oil used to cook the squirrel meat, brown the onions and celery. Add more oil if necessary. Using 2 tablespoons oil and flour, prepare a roux. See roux recipe on page 170. Add roux and return meat to the pot. Add enough water to cover squirrel meat. Add bell pepper and garlic. Bring to a boil, then lower heat, and simmer until meat is tender. Stir in green onions and parsley. Serve hot over rice.

—*Diane*, LOUISIANA

Kofta Curry

Makes 5 to 6 Servings

KOFTAS:
2 small onions, chopped
2 cloves garlic, chopped
1 medium bell pepper, chopped
1 pound ground lamb or lean ground beef
2 teaspoons salt
2 tablespoons ground cumin
1 teaspoon ground ginger
¼ teaspoon ground clove
¼ teaspoon ground cinnamon
¼ teaspoon ground cardamom
¼ –½ teaspoon ground red pepper, to taste
$^1/_8$ teaspoon black pepper
1 egg, beaten
1 cup cooking oil

CURRY:
1 tablespoon cooking oil
1 medium onion, grated
1 teaspoon ground turmeric
1 teaspoon salt
1 teaspoon paprika
1 teaspoon cumin
1 teaspoon coriander
¼ teaspoon red pepper
1 tablespoon plain yogurt
1 cup hot water
Cooked rice, for serving

Koftas: In a medium bowl, combine onions, garlic, bell pepper, and ground meat. Add all seasonings. Knead until mixture is like stiff, smooth dough. Shape into 20–24 meatballs. Heat oil in a large skillet over high heat. Dip each meatball in beaten egg and place in skillet. Cook slowly in deep, hot oil until cooked through.

(continued on next page)

Curry: Heat the cooking oil in a large skillet. Add onion and spices, and sauté for 5 minutes. Add yogurt, and cook an additional 5 minutes. Add the koftas, and cook 5 more minutes, stirring constantly but gently to coat koftas. Add 1 cup of hot water and bring to a boil. Reduce heat, cover, and simmer for 15 minutes. Serve warm with rice.

—*Bela,* LOUISIANA

Grilled Marinated Lamb Chops

Makes 2 Servings

¼ cup white wine
¼ cup white vinegar
¼ cup soy sauce
2 teaspoons honey
2 teaspoons brown sugar
2 cloves garlic, minced
¼ teaspoon cumin
½ teaspoon fresh dill weed, chopped
Black pepper, freshly ground, to taste
4 (1–1½-inch thick) lamb chops, trimmed

Place all ingredients except for lamb chops in a large zip-top bag; stir or shake well. Add chops to bag, shake to coat. Refrigerate for up to 8 hours, turning bag occasionally.

Prepare grill for cooking over medium-hot coals. Remove chops from the bag and grill 5–6 minutes per side, brushing occasionally with marinade.

—*Pastor Dick,* SOUTH CAROLINA

Shish Kabobs

Makes 6 Servings

1 pound ground lamb or beef
1 medium onion, finely chopped
2 cloves garlic, finely chopped
1½ teaspoons salt
2 tablespoons ground coriander
1 teaspoon ground ginger
¼ teaspoon hot red pepper (optional)
¼ teaspoon ground cinnamon
¼ teaspoon ground cloves
¼ teaspoon ground cardamom
1 teaspoon flour
1 teaspoon breadcrumbs
1 tablespoon lemon juice
4 tablespoons yogurt
Mango or apple chutney, for serving

In large bowl combine meat, onion, all spices, flour, breadcrumbs, and lemon juice; mix well. Knead mixture for 10 minutes or until smooth like dough. Divide mixture into 6 equal parts. Wrap each of the 6 portions around a skewer in sausage shape. Brush each liberally with yogurt. Place skewers on broiling pan. Place oven rack 4 inches below broiler and place broiling pan on rack in oven. Set oven to broil and broil for 15–20 minutes, turning every 2–3 minutes. When well browned on all sides, remove skewers from oven and remove meat from skewers. Serve hot with mango or apple chutney.

—*Bela*, LOUISIANA

Lobster-Stuffed Beef Tenderloin

Makes 6 Servings

2 (4-ounce) packages frozen lobster tails
1 (3-pound) beef tenderloin, cut lengthwise
    to within ½-inch of bottom
1 tablespoon butter, melted
1½ teaspoons lemon juice
6 slices bacon
½ cup butter
½ cup green onions, chopped
3 cloves garlic
½ cup dry white wine

Preheat oven to 425°F. Bring a pot of salted water to a boil;
add lobster tails. Cover and simmer 3 minutes. Remove shells
and cut lobster tails in half lengthwise. Place lobster, end to end,
inside the tenderloin. In a small bowl, combine melted butter
with lemon juice; drizzle over lobster. Close the meat and tie with
twine. Roast directly on roasting rack for 30 minutes. Place bacon
on top of roast and bake 5 minutes more.

In a medium saucepan, melt butter, and sauté onion and garlic.
Add wine and cook for another couple of minutes. Serve over roast.

—*Nell,* SOUTH CAROLINA

Peppered Rib-Eyes
with Portobello Sauce

Makes 6 Servings

2½ teaspoons pepper, freshly ground

1½ teaspoons garlic salt

1½ teaspoons lemon pepper

1½ teaspoons ground red pepper

6 (8-ounce) rib-eye steaks

¼ cup olive oil, divided

12 ounces portobello mushrooms

2 cloves garlic, minced

¾ cup red wine

3 small sprigs fresh rosemary

¼ teaspoon salt

¼ teaspoon Italian seasoning

In a small bowl, combine the pepper, garlic salt, lemon pepper, and red pepper. Brush steaks with olive oil; rub with the pepper mixture. Cover and refrigerate for at least 1 hour.

Prepare grill for cooking. Brush the mushrooms with olive oil. Cook on grill until lightly browned. Remove mushrooms from the grill, and set aside. Pour remaining olive oil, about 1 tablespoon, into a large skillet. Add the garlic and cook until lightly browned, about 3 minutes. Add the mushrooms, wine, rosemary, salt, and Italian seasoning. Cook until liquid is reduced, about 10 minutes. Grill the steaks until desired doneness, about 6 minutes per side for medium-rare. Top with the mushroom sauce and serve hot.

—*Josh*, VIRGINIA

Sunday Pot Roast

Makes 5 Servings

1 beef chuck pot roast (about 2½ pounds),
    fat trimmed
Salt, to taste
Black pepper, to taste
2 medium potatoes, scrubbed and quartered
2 large carrots, cut into ¾-inch slices
1 large parsnip, cut into ¾-inch slices
2 large celery stalks, cut into 2-inch pieces
1 medium onion, sliced
2 bay leaves
1 teaspoon dried rosemary
½ teaspoon dried thyme
½ cup beef broth

Cut beef into 5 equal pieces. Season with salt and pepper. Set aside.

Place potatoes, carrots, parsnip, celery, onion, and bay leaves in a slow cooker. Sprinkle with rosemary and thyme. Arrange beef over vegetables. Pour broth over the beef. Cover and cook on low 8½–9 hours or until beef is fork-tender.

Arrange beef and vegetables on a large serving platter. Serve with gravy or juices reserved from the slow cooker.

—Edna, TENNESSEE

Chisholm Trail Pot Roast

Makes 4 to 6 Servings

1 (2–3 pound) chuck roast
½ teaspoon black pepper
½ cup flour, divided
½ cup bacon drippings
1 large onion, sliced
1½ cups beef broth
½ cup coffee
3 carrots, peeled and cut into 2-inch pieces
2 large potatoes, quartered
2 cups water

Sprinkle roast with pepper and dredge in ¼ cup of flour. Heat bacon drippings in a large Dutch oven. Transfer roast to Dutch oven and brown on all sides. Place onions over roast and add beef broth and coffee. Cover and simmer for 1½ hours or until meat is tender. Add carrots and potatoes, cover, and simmer for an additional 30 minutes or until vegetables are tender. Transfer roast and vegetables to a serving platter leaving broth in the Dutch oven. In a small bowl, combine water and remaining ¼ cup of flour; blend until smooth. Pour water/flour mixture into Dutch oven. Cook, stirring constantly, until smooth and thickened. Serve gravy with roast and vegetables.

—*Nanette,* VIRGINIA

Meatballs in Brown Gravy

Makes 6 Servings

1½ pounds lean ground beef
2 slices of white bread, soaked in water,
    excess moisture squeezed out
1½ cups green onions, finely chopped, divided
1 cup onions, finely chopped, divided
⅓ cup bell pepper, finely chopped, divided
⅛ cup parsley, finely chopped
1½ tablespoons garlic, finely chopped
Salt, to taste
Pepper, to taste
2 eggs, lightly beaten
½ cup flour plus 2 tablespoons for roux
¼ cup vegetable oil plus oil for roux
3 cups water
Cooked rice, for serving

In a large bowl, combine ground beef and moist bread. Add half of the green onions, onions, bell pepper, parsley, garlic, salt, and pepper. Mix well. Add lightly beaten eggs to mixture and stir to combine. Shape into meatballs. Place ½ cup of flour in a bowl and dredge meatballs in flour. Heat oil in a skillet. Add meatballs and cook, turning occasionally to brown on all sides. Remove meatballs from skillet and set aside.

Make a roux in the skillet used to brown the meatballs. See recipe on page 170. Add water to the finished roux, the remaining vegetables, parsley, and garlic. Salt and pepper to taste. Add meatballs and bring mixture to a boil. Reduce heat, cover, and simmer for 1 hour. Serve over rice.

—*Marie,* MISSISSIPPI

Swedish Meatballs

Makes 6 Servings

¾ pound ground beef
¾ pound ground pork
1 tablespoon butter
¾ cup onions, chopped
¾ cup soft breadcrumbs
½ cup milk
1 teaspoon salt
¼ teaspoon pepper
¼ teaspoon allspice
1 egg, lightly beaten
¼ cup flour
1½ cups chicken broth
1½ cups half & half
6 cups extra-wide egg noodles, cooked

Combine beef and pork in a large bowl. Melt butter in a large skillet. Add onions to skillet and cook until tender, stirring frequently. Add sautéed onions, breadcrumbs, milk, salt, pepper, allspice, and lightly beaten egg to the meat; mix well. Shape into 1½-inch balls.

Cook meatballs in a large skillet over medium heat, turning occasionally to ensure even browning. Remove meatballs from skillet, reserving 2 tablespoons of the drippings in the pan. Stir in flour and cook, stirring constantly, until mixture is smooth and bubbly. Gradually stir in chicken broth. Cook until mixture boils and thickens, stirring constantly. Stir in half & half; cook an additional 2 minutes. Add meatballs to sauce and simmer 10 minutes, stirring occasionally. Serve meatballs and sauce over hot cooked noodles.

—Stephanie, TENNESSEE

Dirty Rice

Makes 16 Servings

½ pound chicken livers, chopped
1 large onion, finely chopped
3 sprigs parsley, minced
Salt, to taste
Pepper, to taste
1 pound lean ground beef
3 stalks celery, finely chopped
1 pound rice, cooked

Combine all ingredients, except for rice, in a large saucepan and brown over medium-high heat. Reduce heat to medium and sauté, stirring frequently, until livers and ground beef are no longer pink in the middle and juices run clear, about 10 minutes. Add the rice, toss, and cook until heated through.

—*Linda*, NORTH CAROLINA

Indonesian Meat Dish

Makes 6 to 8 Servings

1–1½ pounds ground beef or pork
2 tablespoons oil
1 bundle green onions, only the green parts, finely
    chopped
3–4 apples, diced
2 bell peppers, chopped
3–4 tablespoons sweet soy sauce
1 teaspoon curry powder
3 teaspoons paprika
1 teaspoon ginger powder (or less for less taste)
1 teaspoon garlic powder (or 4 cloves)
½ cube beef bouillon in ½ cup water
3–4 bananas (½ banana for each person), sliced
3–4 cups cooked white rice, for serving

In a large skillet, heat oil, add ground meat and cook until browned.
Add all other ingredients, except the bananas and rice. Simmer
10 minutes. Add bananas and continue to simmer for a 2–3 more
minutes. Serve over white rice.

—*Last Frontier*, MISSISSIPPI

Ginger Beef with Pineapple

Makes 4 to 6 Servings

1 (1-inch) piece fresh ginger,
   cut into very thin strips
1 tablespoon soy sauce
1 tablespoon dry sherry
1 tablespoon cornstarch
1 pound beef tenderloin or top sirloin,
   cut into ¼-inch strips
2 tablespoons canola oil
3 cloves garlic, minced
2 red peppers, seeded and thinly sliced
1 cup pineapple, cut into chunks
½ teaspoon salt
4 green onions, chopped, for garnish
Cooked rice, for serving

In a medium bowl, add ginger, soy sauce, sherry, and cornstarch; stir to combine. Add the beef strips, cover, refrigerate, and marinate for 10 minutes.

Heat the oil in a wok over medium-high heat. Add marinated beef and garlic. Stir-fry for 2 minutes. Add the peppers, pineapple, and salt; stir-fry for 1 minute. Garnish with green onions and serve over hot rice.

—*Sheila*, TENNESSEE

Beef with Broccoli

Makes 2 Servings

½ pound top sirloin, thinly sliced
1 teaspoon saké
1 tablespoon oyster sauce
½ teaspoon sugar
1 tablespoon cornstarch
5 tablespoons canola oil, divided
4 cloves garlic, minced
1 pound fresh broccoli, cut into small florets,
    tough stems discarded
1 tablespoon cornstarch,
    dissolved in ½ cup cold water
1 teaspoon salt
1 teaspoon sesame oil

In a small bowl, mix the beef, saké, oyster sauce, sugar, and cornstarch; set aside. Heat 3 tablespoons of oil in a large wok over high heat. Add sirloin strips to the oil and stir-fry the beef mixture for a few seconds. Remove beef from the wok and set aside. Reduce the wok to low heat and add the remaining 2 tablespoons oil. Add the garlic and broccoli to the wok and stir-fry for 3 minutes. Add the cornstarch mixture, salt, and sesame oil; stir until slightly thickened. Add the cooked beef and mix well. Serve hot.

—*Sheila*, TENNESSEE

Please understand why
Chinese vegetables taste so good.
It is simple:
the Chinese do not cook them,
they just threaten them!

—JEFF SMITH,
The Frugal Gourmet

Easy Sesame Beef

Makes 4 Servings

2 tablespoons sugar
2 tablespoons soy sauce
¼ teaspoon black pepper
¼ cup green onions, finely chopped
2 cloves garlic, finely chopped
1 pound boneless sirloin steak,
    cut diagonally across grain into ⅛-inch slices
1 tablespoon sesame seeds
2 tablespoons vegetable oil
2 cups vermicelli, cooked

In a large bowl, mix sugar, soy sauce, pepper, green onions, and garlic. Add beef and stir until well coated. Cover and refrigerate for 30 minutes.

Toast sesame seeds in a medium skillet, stirring frequently, until golden brown. Remove sesame seeds from skillet. Add oil to the skillet. Drain the beef and add to skillet. Cook, stirring occasionally, until brown. Serve beef over vermicelli. Sprinkle with toasted sesame seeds before serving.

—*Nan,* VIRGINIA

Beef Stroganoff

Makes 4 Servings

4 tablespoons butter, divided
5 tablespoons flour, divided
½ teaspoon salt
1 pound beef sirloin, cut into ¼-inch strips
1 cup mushrooms, thinly sliced
½ medium onion, thinly sliced
1 clove garlic, minced
1 tablespoon tomato paste
1¼ cups beef stock or
    1 (8-ounce) can of beef broth, chilled
1 cup sour cream
3 tablespoons cooking sherry

Melt 2 tablespoons of butter in a skillet over medium-high heat. In a small bowl, mix 1 tablespoon of flour with the salt. Dredge beef strips in flour mixture and place in hot skillet. Brown the sirloin strips quickly. Add sliced mushrooms, onion, and garlic. Cook until onion is slightly tender. Remove meat and mushrooms from skillet; set aside.

Melt remaining 2 tablespoons butter in skillet. Blend in remaining 4 tablespoons of flour. Add tomato paste; stir to combine. Slowly pour in cold beef stock or broth; stir until well blended. Cook until mixture thickens.

Return meat and mushrooms to skillet. Stir in sour cream and sherry. Cook until just heated through.

—Elsie, LOUISIANA

Beef Bologna

Makes 8 Servings

1 cup water
2 tablespoons Morton Tender Quick™ Meat Cure
½ tablespoon liquid smoke
⅛ teaspoon garlic powder
¼ teaspoon onion powder
Dash of red pepper
2 pounds lean ground beef

In a large bowl, combine water, meat cure, and seasonings. Add the ground beef and mix thoroughly. Shape into 3 (3x6-inch) rolls. Wrap meat rolls in clear plastic wrap and refrigerate for 24 hours. (May be frozen at this point.)

Preheat oven to 300°F. Remove meat from refrigerator and discard plastic wrapping. Place in a baking dish and bake for 1 hour. Slice to serve.

—*Gary,* LOUISIANA

Basic Tacos

Makes 12 Tacos

2 tablespoons vegetable oil
1 pound ground beef
1 medium onion, chopped
1½ cups chunky salsa
2 teaspoons Worcestershire sauce
1½ teaspoons chili powder
4 cloves garlic, chopped
½ teaspoon dried oregano
½ teaspoon paprika
¼ teaspoon dried rosemary, crushed
¼ teaspoon ground cumin
Salt, to taste
Pepper, to taste
12 Taco shells
2–3 cups shredded lettuce
2 large tomatoes, chopped
4 ounces Cheddar cheese, shredded

Heat vegetable oil in skillet and add beef and onion. Cover and cook over medium heat until beef is browned. Crumble beef and drain. Stir in salsa and seasonings.

Heat Taco shells according to package directions. Place 2–3 tablespoons of meat into each shell. Top with lettuce, tomatoes, and cheese.

—*Marie*, MISSISSIPPI

Open-Faced Burgers with Onion-Mushroom Topping

Makes 4 Servings

2 teaspoons olive oil
1 medium sweet onion, sliced and
    separated into rings
16 ounces mushrooms, sliced
½ teaspoon salt
2 teaspoons balsamic vinegar
1½ teaspoons paprika
½ teaspoon black pepper
½ teaspoon dried thyme
¼ teaspoon ground red pepper
1 pound ground round
2 English muffins

Prepare grill for cooking. Heat oil in a large nonstick skillet over medium heat. Add onion, and cook for 5 minutes or until golden brown. Add mushrooms and salt; cook for 5 minutes, stirring constantly. Stir in vinegar. Remove from heat and set aside.

In a very small bowl or a cup, mix paprika, black pepper, thyme, and red pepper. Divide the ground round into 4 equal portions, shaping each into a ½-inch thick patty. Coat the patties with the spice mixture.

Transfer patties to grill and cook 4 minutes on each side or until cooked to desired doneness. Place burgers on muffin halves and top with ¼ cup of onion mixture.

—*Peggy*, NORTH CAROLINA

Barbecued Brisket

You can make a delicious sauce using the brisket's drippings. Simply degrease the drippings. Pour drippings into a small saucepan with a cup or so of wine, beer, or water. Simmer until the sauce thickens. Pour the sauce over the sliced brisket and enjoy!

Makes 14 to 18 Servings

7–9 pounds beef brisket
1 rounded teaspoon garlic, minced
1 teaspoon celery seeds
3 tablespoons freshly ground pepper
1 teaspoon ground ginger
4 large bay leaves, crumbled
1 (12-ounce) can tomato paste
½ cup Worcestershire sauce
1 cup dark soy sauce
1 cup brown sugar, packed
2 medium onions, thinly sliced

Preheat over to 350°F. Rub all sides of the brisket with garlic. Place on heavy-duty aluminum foil. In a small bowl, combine celery seeds, pepper, ginger, and bay leaves. Sprinkle spice/herb mixture on all sides of the meat. In a small bowl, mix tomato paste, Worcestershire sauce, soy sauce, and brown sugar; rub on meat. Score the fat side of the brisket and place onions on top. Wrap in foil and seal tightly. Place fat side up in a roasting pan and cook for 4 hours. Open the foil to expose onions and cook for another hour.

—*Debbie,* ARKANSAS

Jesse's Barbeque Dipping Sauce
(For Pork or Chicken)

Sauce can be frozen

Makes 2 Cups

½ cup finely chopped onion
¼ stick (¹/₈ cup) butter
2 tablespoons vinegar
¾ cup ketchup
3 tablespoons brown sugar
2 tablespoons molasses
3 tablespoons Worcestershire sauce
1 teaspoon dry mustard
1 teaspoon salt
¼ teaspoon paprika
¼ teaspoon garlic salt
½ teaspoon black pepper

In a medium pot, sauté onion and butter. Add remaining ingredients and simmer for about 15 minutes. Serve warm. Refrigerate after serving.

—*Jesse,* MISSISSIPPI

Jezebel Sauce
(For Ham)

Makes 5 Cups

1 (18-ounce) jar pineapple preserves
1 (18-ounce) jar apple jelly
1 (5-ounce) jar horseradish
1 (1½-ounce) can dry mustard
1 tablespoon cracked black pepper (optional)

Combine all ingredients in a blender or food processor. Process until sauce is smooth. Store in the refrigerator for up to 3 weeks.

—*Wyonnie*, GEORGIA

Peach Salsa
(For Chicken, Pork, or Fish)

Makes 2 Cups

1½ tablespoons lime juice
¼ cup hot pepper jelly
½ cup red onion, minced
⅓ cup green bell pepper, chopped
⅓ cup red bell pepper, chopped
2 tablespoons fresh cilantro, chopped
3 ripe peaches, pitted and finely diced

In a small bowl, add lime juice and pepper jelly; whisk to combine. Add onion, peppers, and cilantro. Mix well. Add peaches and stir to coat. Cover and refrigerate for at least 30 minutes before serving. Fresh mango may be substituted for the peaches.

—*Linda*, NORTH CAROLINA

John's Remoulade Sauce
(For Seafood)

Makes 1½ to 2 Cups

1 cup mayonnaise
1 tablespoon onion, chopped
1 tablespoon vinegar
1 teaspoon paprika
1 tablespoon fresh parsley, chopped
½ teaspoon salt (optional)
2–3 drops Tabasco™ sauce
2 tablespoons Creole mustard
1 tablespoon horseradish
¼ cup celery, chopped
1 teaspoon Worcestershire sauce
¼ cup olive oil

Combine all ingredients in a blender or food processor. Blend until thoroughly mixed. Serve with your favorite seafood.

—*Fay*, MISSISSIPPI

Beer Sauce
(For Fish)

Makes 3 Cups

1 (1½-ounce) can dry mustard
¾–1 cup beer
2 cups mayonnaise
1 tablespoon Worcestershire sauce
1 tablespoon Louisiana hot sauce
1 small onion, grated

In a mixing bowl, add dry mustard and enough beer to make a creamy, but not runny, paste. Add mayonnaise and stir to combine. Add Worcestershire sauce, hot sauce, and onion; mix well. Taste, and if you would prefer a milder flavor, add additional mayonnaise. Refrigerate at least 20 minutes before serving.

—*Jackie*, LOUISIANA

Roux

Heat oil in a large skillet over medium-low heat. Slowly stir in flour until the mixture forms a thick paste. Cook, stirring constantly with a wooden spoon, until the mixture reaches your desired shade of brown, no lighter than pale golden, and no darker than dark chocolate. This should take at least 30 minutes. Don't try to rush the cooking by turning up the heat—roux is very easy to burn.

—*Thelma June*, ALABAMA

Sausage Gravy

Makes 6 Cups

1 pound sage-flavored bulk pork sausage
2 tablespoons onion, finely chopped
6 tablespoons flour
4 cups milk
½ teaspoon poultry seasoning
½ teaspoon ground nutmeg
¼ teaspoon salt
Dash Worcestershire sauce
Dash hot sauce

In a large skillet over medium-low heat, brown sausage and crumble sausage. Add onion and cook, stirring often, until onion is translucent. Drain and discard all but about 2 tablespoons of sausage drippings. Stir in flour and cook 6 additional minutes or until the mixture bubbles and turns golden. Stir in milk. Add poultry seasoning, nutmeg, salt, Worcestershire sauce, and hot sauce. Cook, stirring frequently, until sauce thickens. Serve hot over sliced biscuits.

—*Sylvia*, ARKANSAS

Side Dishes

The discovery of a new dish
does more for the happiness of mankind
than the discovery of a new star.

—JEAN-ANTHELME BRILLAT-SAVARIN

Green Beans with Almond Sauce

Makes 6 Servings

GREEN BEANS:
4 tablespoons olive oil
1 medium onion, chopped
1 teaspoon bacon bits
4 cups (2 14½-ounce cans) green beans
Salt, to taste
Pepper, to taste

SAUCE:
1 cup salad dressing
2 eggs, hard-boiled, chopped
¾ cup slivered almonds, toasted
1 teaspoon parsley flakes
Juice of 1 lemon

Green Beans: In large skillet, heat oil and add onion, bacon bits, and green beans; stir to combine. Cook for 20 minutes. Season with salt and pepper. Drain beans.

Sauce: In a medium bowl, combine all sauce ingredients and mix well. Spoon over beans, and serve.

—*Barbara,* LOUISIANA

Scalloped Zucchini

Makes 6 to 8 Servings

4 tablespoons butter, melted, divided
1 small onion, sliced
4 medium zucchini or yellow squash, sliced
2 firm tomatoes, cut into wedges
2 teaspoons sugar
1 teaspoon salt
¼ teaspoon oregano
⅛ teaspoon pepper
2 tablespoons Parmesan cheese, grated

Preheat oven to 350°F. In a shallow 6-cup baking dish, combine 2 tablespoons melted butter and sliced onion. Add zucchini or squash slices and tomato wedges. In small bowl, combine sugar, salt, oregano, and pepper; sprinkle over mixture in baking dish. Drizzle with remaining 2 tablespoons of melted butter. Bake for 1 hour. Sprinkle with Parmesan cheese before serving.

—*Zachary*, VIRGINIA

Parmesan Zucchini

Makes 10 to 12 Servings

5 medium zucchini, very thinly sliced
2 tablespoons butter
Garlic salt, to taste
¾ cup Parmesan cheese, grated

Melt butter in a large skillet and sauté zucchini slices until just tender. Sprinkle zucchini with garlic salt and cheese; stir to coat. Increase heat and cook until cheese is melted and golden brown. Serve warm.

—*Kristin*, SOUTH CAROLINA

Fried Okra & Eggplant

Makes 4 Servings

1 cup okra, cut into ½-inch slices
1 cup eggplant, cut into ½-inch cubes
Salt, to taste
Pepper, to taste
¼ cup cornmeal
Vegetable oil, for frying

In a large bowl, combine sliced okra and cubed eggplant. Add salt and pepper, to taste. Sprinkle cornmeal on vegetable mixture. Heat oil in a non-stick skillet. Transfer vegetable mixture to skillet and fry, turning frequently. Cook for about 10 minutes or until lightly browned.

—*Alicia*, ARKANSAS

Ratatouille

Makes 6 Servings

¼ cup olive oil
1½ pounds eggplant, cubed
½ pound zucchini, cubed
1 cup green bell pepper, chopped
½ cup medium onion, finely chopped
2 medium tomatoes, quartered
1½ teaspoons salt
¼ teaspoon pepper
1 clove garlic, crushed

Heat oil in a 12-inch skillet. Add vegetables and stir. Add garlic and sprinkle with salt and pepper. Cook over medium heat for 10–15 minutes, stirring occasionally, until zucchini is tender.

—*Cecelia*, NORTH CAROLINA

Gourmet Baked Acorn Squash

Makes 6 Servings

3 acorn squash, halved and seeded
$^2/_3$ cup celery, diced
1½ cups apples, diced
¼ cup butter
1½ cups soft breadcrumbs
1 cup cheese, shredded
½ teaspoon salt
$^1/_8$ teaspoon pepper

Preheat oven to 400°F. Place squash halves, cut side down, in baking pan in a small amount of water. Bake 20–30 minutes, or until almost tender.

In a medium skillet, melt butter, and sauté celery and apples for 5 minutes. Stir in breadcrumbs, cheese, salt, and pepper.

Turn squash halves over; fill with apple mixture. Bake 10–15 minutes longer or until squash halves are tender.

—*Ester,* GEORGIA

Stewed Collards and Salt Pork

Makes 6 Servings

½ pound salt pork or slab bacon,
    cut into small cubes
2 onions, sliced
2 pounds collard greens
Salt, to taste
Pepper, to taste
½ cup water

In a large skillet or pot, cook pork until crisp. Remove meat and discard one half of the drippings. Sauté the onions in remaining drippings until tender. Wash collard greens thoroughly and remove tough stems and ribs. Cut greens to desired size. Add collards, salt, pepper, and water to onions. Cook covered over low heat for 15 minutes or until collards are tender. Add a little more water, if needed. Return meat to cooked greens; heat through, and serve immediately.

—In loving memory of Betsy, ARKANSAS

Browned Turnips

Makes 4 Servings

8 turnips
2 cups chicken stock
3–4 tablespoons butter
3–4 tablespoons brown sugar
Salt, to taste
Pepper, to taste

Peel and cube turnips. In a medium pan, place turnips in chicken stock and boil until slightly tender. Do not over cook. Heat butter in a separate skillet. Add partially cooked cubes of turnips and sprinkle with brown sugar. Turn turnips once to brown on both sides. Add salt and pepper to taste. To keep warm, add 2 tablespoons of hot water and cover until serving time.

—Anne and Marilyn, KENTUCKY

German Red Cabbage

Makes 4 to 6 Servings

1 tablespoon vegetable oil
1 medium onion, chopped
1 medium head red cabbage, coarsely chopped
½ teaspoon salt
1 tablespoon sugar
1 tablespoon red wine vinegar
2–3 tart apples, sliced

Heat oil in small skillet, add onions and sauté until tender. In a large pot, add water until the depth is ½-inch in the bottom of the pot. Bring water to a boil. Add cabbage, onions, salt, sugar, and vinegar; mix well. Reduce heat to medium and steam cabbage for about 20 minutes. Stir apple slices into cabbage, and cook for another 30 minutes.

This recipe can also be made in a crockpot, taking 4–6 hours to cook cabbage. Add apples during the last hour of cooking.

—*Linda*, NORTH CAROLINA

Spicy Sweet-and-Sour Cabbage

Makes 8 Servings

2 tablespoons sugar
½ teaspoon salt
2 tablespoons soy sauce
2 tablespoons white vinegar
3 tablespoons peanut oil
½ teaspoon crushed red pepper or
    4 whole dried red peppers, crushed
6 cups cabbage (1 small head)
    cut into 1-inch squares

In a small bowl, combine sugar, salt, soy sauce, and vinegar. Set aside. Heat wok over high heat for 30 seconds. Add peanut oil, and reduce heat to medium. Add red pepper and stir-fry 5 seconds. Add cabbage; stir-fry 5 minutes. Stir the soy sauce mixture and pour over cabbage. Turn heat to high. Stir until well mixed. Serve immediately.

—*Sylvia,* LOUISIANA

Part of the secret of success in life is to eat what you like and let the food fight it out inside.

—MARK TWAIN

Hot Cabbage Creole

Makes 6 Servings

1 tablespoon butter
1 large onion, chopped
1 large green pepper, chopped
2 slices bacon, cut into 1-inch pieces
1 (28-ounce) can whole tomatoes
1 head cabbage, finely chopped
2 teaspoons salt
½ teaspoon black pepper
¼ teaspoon cayenne pepper
⅓ cup vinegar

In a heavy saucepan, melt butter and sauté onion, green pepper, and bacon. Add tomatoes, cabbage, salt, peppers, and vinegar. Bring mixture to a boil. Reduce heat and cover. Simmer for 45–55 minutes, or until cabbage is cooked to desired consistency.

—*Margaret,* MISSISSIPPI

Dill Marinated Vegetables

Makes 8 Servings

VEGETABLES:
2 bunches broccoli
1 head cauliflower
2 cups (1 pint) mushrooms

MARINADE:
1 cup apple cider vinegar
1 tablespoon sugar
1 tablespoon dill weed
1 teaspoon salt
1 teaspoon pepper
1 teaspoon garlic salt
1½ cups vegetable oil

Vegetables: Wash the vegetables thoroughly. Break or cut into bite size pieces and place in a large bowl; set aside.

Marinade: In medium bowl, combine all marinade ingredients; stir until well mixed. Pour marinade over vegetables. Cover and refrigerate vegetables for 24 hours to allow flavors to blend, stirring occasionally. Serve cold.

—*Joan,* SOUTH CAROLINA

Roasted Cauliflower

Makes 6 Servings

6 cups cauliflower (1 large head),
    separated into flowerets
3 tablespoons olive oil
1 teaspoon minced garlic packed in olive oil
½ teaspoon curry powder
½ teaspoon ground cumin
½ teaspoon dried basil, crushed
½ teaspoon dry mustard
¼ teaspoon salt

Preheat oven to 450°F. Place cauliflower in a 2-quart rectangular baking dish. In a small bowl, combine olive oil, minced garlic, curry powder, cumin, basil, mustard, and salt. Drizzle over cauliflower, tossing to coat.

Bake for 30 minutes or until lightly toasted, stirring gently after 15 minutes. Serve hot.

—*Stephanie*, TENNESSEE

Cucumbers in Sour Cream

Makes 6 Servings

5 cucumbers, peeled and thinly sliced
¼ teaspoon salt
½ teaspoon pepper
2 tablespoons white vinegar
8 ounces sour cream
1 tablespoon fresh dill, chopped

Place cucumber slices in a flat-bottomed, shallow container. Sprinkle with salt and pepper. In a small bowl, combine sour cream and vinegar; mix well. Pour sour cream mixture over cucumbers. Sprinkle the dill weed on top, and serve while flavors are fresh.

—*Wilma*, KENTUCKY

Fried Green Tomatoes

Makes 8 to 10 Servings

6–8 green tomatoes
1 cup self-rising flour
½ cup cornmeal
½ teaspoon salt
1 egg, beaten
1 cup milk or buttermilk
Bacon drippings or vegetable oil, for frying

Cut the tomatoes into ½-inch slices; set aside. In a bowl, mix flour, cornmeal, and salt; set aside. In a shallow baking dish, combine beaten egg and milk or buttermilk. Dip tomato slices into the egg mixture allowing the excess liquid to drip back into the dish. Coat the egg-dipped tomato slices with flour mixture. In a large heavy skillet, fry coated tomato slices in hot oil turning once until browned on both sides. Transfer to colander to drain.

—*Peggy*, ALABAMA

Tomatoes Del-Mar

Makes 8 Servings

SEASONED BREADCRUMBS:
1 package cornbread mix
½ teaspoon lemon pepper
Celery salt, to taste
Garlic salt, to taste
¼ teaspoon cayenne pepper
Dash of black pepper

(continued on next page)

TOMATOES:

2 tablespoons butter

1 tablespoon olive oil

½ cup onion, chopped

½ cup celery, chopped

½ cup bell pepper, chopped

1 (28-ounce) can tomatoes, diced

¼ cup sugar (optional)

¼ cup brown sugar

3 tablespoons dried basil

4 tablespoons cornstarch

2 tablespoons balsamic vinegar or apple cider vinegar

¼ teaspoon lemon pepper

¼ teaspoon garlic salt

2 teaspoons seasoned salt

½ teaspoon black pepper, or to taste

¼ cup butter, melted

Seasoned Breadcrumbs: Preheat oven temperature according to cornbread package directions. In a medium bowl, whisk cornbread mix and all breadcrumb seasonings. Bake according to cornbread package directions. Cool, crumble, and set aside.

Tomatoes: Preheat oven to 350°F. In a large skillet, add butter and olive oil. Add chopped onion, celery, and bell pepper; sauté until onions are tender. Add tomatoes, sugars, and basil; stir to combine. In small bowl, mix cornstarch and vinegar; stir into tomato mixture. Bring to a boil. Add lemon pepper, garlic salt, seasoned salt, and black pepper; stir.

Pour into greased 2-quart casserole dish. Sprinkle seasoned breadcrumbs over casserole and pour melted butter on top of the breadcrumbs. Bake for 30–45 minutes, or until filling is bubbly, and breadcrumbs are lightly browned.

—*Marie,* MISSISSIPPI

Tomato Pie

Makes 8 Servings

1 deep-dish pie crust, baked
4–5 tomatoes
1 large Vidalia onion, chopped
½ teaspoon salt
½ teaspoon garlic powder
½ teaspoon basil
¼ teaspoon pepper
¼ teaspoon oregano
1 cup Cheddar cheese, shredded
1 cup mayonnaise
4 slices bacon, cooked and crumbled

Cut the tomatoes into ⅛-inch slices. In a large bowl, combine the sliced tomatoes and onion. Add salt, garlic powder, basil, pepper, and oregano to tomatoes and onion. Mix and refrigerate for 1 hour. Preheat oven to 350°F. In a separate bowl, combine shredded cheese and mayonnaise. Using a slotted spoon to drain liquid, transfer tomato mixture into the baked piecrust. Spread mayonnaise mixture on top. Sprinkle cooked and crumbled bacon over the mayonnaise mixture. Bake for 40–50 minutes.

—*Kathleen*, ALABAMA

Fire and Ice Tomatoes

Makes 6 to 8 Servings

6 medium tomatoes, peeled, quartered, and seeded
1 medium onion, sliced
1 medium green pepper, cut in strips
1 large cucumber, sliced
¾ cup cider vinegar
¼ cup water
1 tablespoon plus 2 teaspoons sugar
1½ teaspoons celery salt
½ teaspoon red pepper flakes
1½ teaspoons mustard seed
$\frac{1}{8}$ teaspoon black pepper

In a large bowl, combine quartered tomatoes, sliced onion, green pepper strips, and sliced cucumber. Set aside. In a small saucepan, add vinegar, water, sugar, celery salt, red pepper flakes, mustard seed, and black pepper; stir to combine. Bring to a boil and cook for 1 minute. Pour liquid over vegetables. Cover and chill for 8 hours to allow vegetables to absorb marinade.

—*Roy,* NORTH CAROLINA

It's difficult to think anything but pleasant thoughts while eating a homegrown tomato.

—LEWIS GRIZZARD

Bloomin' Onion

Makes 4 Servings

ONIONS:
4 Vidalia or Texas Sweet Onions

SEASONED FLOUR:
2 cups flour
4 teaspoons paprika
2 teaspoons garlic powder
½ teaspoon pepper
¼ teaspoon cayenne pepper

BATTER:
½ cup cornstarch
1½ cups flour
2 teaspoons garlic, minced
2 teaspoons paprika
1 teaspoon salt
1 teaspoon pepper
3 cups (24-ounces) beer

CREAMY CHILI SAUCE:
2 cups (1 pint) mayonnaise
2 tablespoons sour cream
½ cup chili sauce
½ teaspoon cayenne pepper

Onions: Cut about ¾-inch off the top of each onion and peel. Make 12–16 vertical cuts into each onion, but do not cut through the bottom root end. Remove about 1-inch of petals from center of onion.

Seasoned Flour: In a medium bowl, add the 5 seasoned flour ingredients and whisk to combine. Dip onions in seasoned flour; shake to remove excess.

(continued on next page)

Batter: Heat oil in deep-fat fryer to 375°F–400°F. In a small bowl, combine cornstarch, flour, and seasonings. Add beer and mix well. Dip onions in batter to coat thoroughly. Gently place in fryer basket and deep fry for 1½ minutes. Turn over and fry for an additional 1½ minutes. Drain on paper towels.

Creamy Chili Sauce: In small bowl, add all chili sauce ingredients; stir until blended.

Serve chili sauce with the onions.

—*Christy,* NORTH CAROLINA

Vidalia Onion Pie

Makes 6 Servings

3 eggs, beaten
1 cup sour cream
1½ teaspoons brown sugar
1½ teaspoons maple syrup
3 cups Vidalia onions, sliced
1 tablespoon vanilla
Salt, to taste
Pepper, to taste
1 pie shell, unbaked
1 cup cheese (of your choice), grated

Preheat oven to 350°F. In large bowl, combine beaten eggs, sour cream, brown sugar, and maple syrup; mix thoroughly. Add onions and toss to coat. Stir in vanilla, salt, and pepper. Pour onion mixture into pie shell and sprinkle with cheese. Bake for 45–60 minutes or until cheese browns and pie is cooked through.

—*Linda,* SOUTH CAROLINA

Corn Pudding

Makes 4 Servings

1 cup corn
3 eggs, well beaten
3 tablespoons sugar
1 teaspoon flour
1 cup cream
½ teaspoon baking powder
Salt and pepper, to taste

Preheat oven to 350°F. Combine all ingredients and pour into lightly greased casserole dish. Place dish in a shallow pan of water, transfer to oven and bake for 1 hour or until toothpick inserted in center of pudding comes out clean.

—*Rosa*, ALABAMA

Hominy Casserole

Makes 4 to 5 Servings

2 (16-ounce) cans white hominy, drained
1 (4-ounce) can chopped green chili peppers;
    drained with 1 tablespoon of juice reserved
1 small onion, grated
1 cup sour cream
1 cup mozzarella cheese, grated
½ teaspoon salt
Paprika or parsley flakes, for garnish

Preheat oven to 350°F. In a large bowl, combine hominy, chili peppers, 1 tablespoon of chili pepper juice, onion, sour cream, cheese, and salt; mix well. Pour into casserole dish. Cover and bake for 30 minutes. Sprinkle top with paprika or parsley flakes.

—*Mildred*, ARKANSAS

Hoppin' John

*Serve with Collard Greens for a Traditional
and Lucky Southern New Year's Meal*

Makes 8 to 10 Servings

1 pound (2 cups) dried black-eyed peas
6 cups cold water
1 medium onion, sliced
2 teaspoons salt
¼ pound lean salt pork, sliced
2 cups rice, cooked

Wash peas and place in a large pot. Add cold water. Bring to a
boil and boil for 2 minutes. Remove from heat, cover pot, and
let stand for 1 hour. Do not drain. Add onion, salt, and salt pork
to the peas and boil gently until peas are soft, about 1 hour. Add
cooked rice and simmer for 10 minutes to allow flavors to blend.

—*C. J.*, GEORGIA

**Eat a serving of Hoppin' John on New
Year's Day** and good luck and wealth will
be yours in the year to come. With origins from
Lowcountry rice plantations, this dish is a hearty
combination of black-eyed peas, salt pork or
slab bacon, white rice, and seasonings and is
often accompanied by collard greens. Southern
lore holds that the peas with little black "eyes"
signify coins. Rice swells while cooking offering
abundance. Pork is not just for flavoring. Hogs
can't look back, so pork represents the future.
Partner up your Hoppin' John with collard greens
to symbolize dollar bills bringing prosperity.

Wild Black Beans

Makes 4 Servings

2 cups wild rice, cooked
1 (15-ounce) can black beans, undrained
1 cup corn, drained
½ cup red bell pepper, chopped
1 small jalapeño pepper, seeded and chopped
1 tablespoon red wine vinegar
1 cup Monterey Jack cheese, shredded
¼ cup fresh cilantro, chopped

Preheat oven to 350°F. In a 1½-quart baking dish, add cooked rice, beans, corn, bell pepper, jalapeño pepper, and wine vinegar; stir to combine. Cover and bake for 20 minutes. Top with cheese; bake uncovered for 10 minutes. Garnish with cilantro.

—*Jennifer,* NORTH CAROLINA

Delicious Baked Beans

Makes 6 to 8 Servings

1 pound ground beef
½ pound bacon
2–3 (16-ounce) cans pork and beans
1 cup brown sugar
1 teaspoon mustard
1 onion, finely chopped
1 clove garlic, finely chopped
1 bell pepper, finely chopped
½ jalapeño pepper, chopped (optional)
1 cup ketchup

Preheat oven to 350°F. In a large pan, cook ground beef until just slightly pink. Drain grease. Cut bacon into 1-inch strips. Add bacon to ground beef in pan and cook until ground beef is browned and bacon is cooked through. Add remaining ingredients; mix well. Transfer to casserole dish. Bake for 30 minutes.

—*Melinda,* MISSISSIPPI

Country Barbecued Beans

Makes 14 to 16 Servings

1 (16-ounce) can pork and beans
1 (16-ounce) can kidney beans
1 (16-ounce) can pinto beans
1 (16-ounce) can Northern beans
1 (16-ounce) can butter beans
1 (16-ounce) can navy beans
8 strips bacon
¼ cup barbecue sauce
¼ cup mustard
⅓ cup ketchup
1 cup brown sugar
½ cup honey or molasses
1 medium onion, finely chopped
1 sweet pepper (red or green), finely chopped

Preheat oven to 450°F. Mix all ingredients in a 5-quart baking pan. Top with bacon strips. Bake until bacon is cooked through, about 30–45 minutes.

—*Terri*, NORTH CAROLINA

Old-Fashioned Baked Beans with Spices

Makes 6 Servings

1 (31-ounce) can pork and beans
1 teaspoon dry mustard
1 tablespoon prepared mustard
$\frac{1}{8}$ teaspoon pepper
2 teaspoons salt
¼ cup brown sugar
1 green bell pepper, chopped
1 large onion, finely diced
1 tablespoon sweet pickle juice
$\frac{1}{8}$ teaspoon ground cinnamon
$\frac{1}{8}$ teaspoon ground cloves
¼ cup ketchup
Juice of ½ lemon
2 tablespoons barbeque sauce
1 tablespoon Worcestershire sauce
6 slices bacon, fried and crumbled

Preheat oven to 300°F. In a large bowl, combine all ingredients except the bacon. Stir gently until thoroughly combined, being careful not to mash the beans. Pour into a casserole dish and bake uncovered for 2 hours. Place crumbled bacon on top for the last 30 minutes of baking.

—*Kathy,* MISSISSIPPI

Suzi's Block Party Beans

Makes 20 to 25 Servings

For a Crowd

1 pound pork sausage

1 (16-ounce) can wax beans

1 (16-ounce) can green beans

1 (16-ounce) can lima beans

1 (16-ounce) can kidney beans

1 (16-ounce) can chili beans

1 (46-ounce) can pork and beans

1 (6-ounce) can tomato paste

1 (10¾-ounce) can tomato soup

½ cup barbecue sauce

½ cup brown sugar

4–6 strips bacon, more if desired

Preheat oven to 350°F. In a frying pan, brown and drain sausage. Drain wax, green, lima, and kidney beans. In a large bowl, combine all beans including liquid from chili beans and pork and beans. In a small bowl, mix tomato paste, tomato soup, barbecue sauce, and brown sugar. Add cooked sausage and sauce mixture from small bowl to the beans and stir. Pour into a lightly greased 9x13-inch glass baking dish. Cover with bacon strips. Bake for 1 hour and 45 minutes.

—*Willa*, ALABAMA

Red Savannah Rice

Makes 8 to 10 Servings

½ pound bacon, sliced

½ cup onion, chopped

2 cups rice, uncooked, rinsed several times

2 cups stewed red tomatoes with juice

2½ cups water

½ teaspoon salt

¼ teaspoon pepper

⅛ teaspoon hot pepper sauce (optional)

Preheat oven to 350°F. In a large skillet, fry bacon until crisp. Do not drain grease. Remove bacon from pan and crumble. Add onions to bacon drippings in pan; cook onions until tender. Add rinsed rice, stewed tomatoes with juice, water, salt, pepper, hot pepper sauce if desired, and crumbled bacon. Cook over low heat for about 10 minutes. Pour mixture into a 2-quart casserole. Cover tightly. Place in oven and bake for 1 hour. Stir with a fork several times during baking. Add a little water if the rice seems too dry.

—*Marie*, GEORGIA

Spicy Rice Pilaf

Makes 6 to 8 Servings

½ cup onion, chopped
2 tablespoons olive or vegetable oil
2 cups chicken broth
¼ cup dried lentils, rinsed
1 (16-ounce) can kidney beans, drained
1 cup salsa
1 cup long-grain rice, uncooked
1 cup frozen shoepeg corn
1 (2-ounce) jar diced pimentos, drained
1 teaspoon chili powder

In saucepan over medium heat, sauté onion in oil until tender. Add broth and lentils; bring to a boil. Reduce heat, cover, and simmer for 15 minutes. Stir in remaining ingredients. Bring to a boil. Reduce heat, cover, and simmer for 20–25 minutes or until lentils are nice and tender.

—*Patsy,* KENTUCKY

*If more of us valued food
and cheer and song
above hoarded gold,
it would be a merrier world.*

—J.R.R. TOLKIEN

Brown Rice and Vegetables

Makes 4 Servings

1 cup brown rice
1 cup chicken broth
1$^2/_3$ cups water
2 tablespoons butter
1 cup onion, cut into large strips
1 cup green peppers, cut into large strips
1 yellow squash, sliced into ¼-inch thick circles
8 mushrooms, quartered
10 cherry tomatoes, halved
Salt, to taste
Pepper, to taste

Combine rice, broth, and water in a large saucepan; bring to a boil. Cover, reduce heat, and simmer for 50 minutes or until moisture is absorbed and rice is tender.

In a large skillet, melt butter; add onion, green pepper, and squash and sauté for 3–4 minutes. Add mushrooms and tomatoes; cook until just heated through. Add cooked rice to skillet. Stir gently until well combined. Serve warm.

—*Marie,* MISSISSIPPI

Beverly's Turkish Rice Pilaf

Makes 6 Servings

2 cups rice, uncooked
1 medium onion, finely chopped
1–1½ tablespoons butter
¼ cup of peanuts
4 cups chicken stock
¼ cup of raisins
Parsley flakes, to taste
Dash of cinnamon
Dash of nutmeg, freshly ground
Dash of ground cloves
Salt, to taste
Pepper, to taste

Soak rice in salted, warm water for 15 minutes; drain and set aside.
In large saucepan, sauté onion in butter until lightly browned.
Add peanuts and rice. Sauté until nuts are lightly browned. Add
all other ingredients and cook until rice is tender or all liquid is
absorbed. Toss lightly to mix. Serve warm.

This is a modified Turkish recipe. Bite-sized pieces of cooked
chicken can be added just before the liquid is added to cook the
rice. The Turks also add tomato.

—*Beverly*, LOUISIANA

Barley and Pine Nuts

Makes 4 to 6 Servings

1 cup pearl barley
6 tablespoons butter, divided
½ cup pine nuts, slivered almonds,
   or chopped pecans
1 onion, chopped
½ cup fresh parsley, minced
¼ teaspoon salt
¼ teaspoon pepper
3½ cups beef broth

Preheat oven to 375°F. Rinse the barley in cold water, drain well, and set aside. In a large skillet, melt 2 tablespoons butter; add nuts and stir until lightly toasted. Transfer nuts to a small bowl and set aside. Melt remaining 4 tablespoons of butter in skillet. Add onion and drained barley; cook and stir until onions are tender and barley is lightly toasted. Remove from heat. Stir in nuts, parsley, salt, and pepper. Spoon into 1½- quart baking dish. Heat broth, and pour over barley mixture. Bake uncovered for about 1 hour and 10 minutes.

—*Nancy,* SOUTH CAROLINA

Summer Vegetable Spaghetti

Makes 8 to 10 Servings

2 cups small yellow onions, cut in eighths

2 cups fresh ripe tomatoes (about 1 pound),
    peeled and chopped

2 cups yellow and green squash (about 1 pound),
    thinly sliced

1½ cups fresh green beans (about ½ pound)

²/₃ cup water

2 tablespoons fresh parsley, minced

1 clove garlic, minced

½ teaspoon chili powder

¼ teaspoon salt

Black pepper, to taste

1 (6-ounce) can tomato paste

1 pound spaghetti, uncooked

½ cup Parmesan cheese, grated

In a large saucepan, add the first 10 ingredients; stir gently to combine. Cook for 10 minutes over medium heat. Stir in the tomato paste. Reduce heat to low. Cover and cook for 15 minutes, stirring occasionally, until vegetables are tender. Cook spaghetti in unsalted water according to package directions. Drain. Spoon the sauce over hot spaghetti. Sprinkle with Parmesan cheese and serve.

—Mary, LOUISIANA

Penne Pasta with Asparagus

Makes 4 to 6 Servings

CARAMELIZED ONIONS:
3 tablespoons butter
3 tablespoons olive oil
2 medium to large yellow onions, sliced
1 teaspoon brown sugar

ASPARAGUS:
1 pound fresh asparagus, trimmed
    and cut into 2-inch diagonal slices
1 cup olive oil
1 clove garlic, thinly sliced or crushed
½ tablespoon kosher salt

FOR SERVING:
¾ pound penne pasta, cooked
¾ cup Parmesan cheese

Caramelized Onions: In a skillet, heat 3 tablespoons each of butter and olive oil. Add onions and brown sugar; stir to coat. Cook 20–30 minutes over medium-low heat, stirring frequently.

Asparagus: Preheat oven to 500°F. Place asparagus, 1 cup of olive oil, garlic, and salt in a baking dish. Roast on top rack of oven for 10–15 minutes. Shake pan 2 or 3 times during baking.

For Serving: Combine asparagus, onions, and cooked pasta in serving bowl. Toss with Parmesan cheese and serve.

—*Courtney,* SOUTH CAROLINA

Baked Macaroni and Cheese

Makes 8 to 10 Servings

1 (16-ounce) package large elbow macaroni
½ cup butter
½ cup flour
2 cups milk
3 cups Cheddar cheese, shredded and divided
1 (12-ounce) carton small-curd cottage cheese
2 large eggs, lightly beaten
1 teaspoon salt
½ cup breadcrumbs
1 teaspoon Greek seasoning

Preheat oven to 350ºF. Cook pasta according to package directions; drain. Melt butter in a Dutch oven over low heat; whisk in flour until smooth. Continue to whisk while gradually adding milk. Cook over medium heat until mixture is thick and bubbly. Stir in 2 cups Cheddar cheese, cottage cheese, beaten eggs, and salt. Stir in cooked pasta. Spoon mixture into a lightly greased 13x9-inch baking dish. Top with remaining 1 cup of Cheddar cheese. In a small bowl, combine breadcrumbs and Greek seasoning; sprinkle mixture over cheese. Bake for 25 minutes.

—*Laura*, MISSISSIPPI

Macaroni and Cheese

For a Crowd

Serve for Lenten Luncheon
Makes 50 Servings

2½ pounds macaroni, uncooked
5 sticks (1 pound 4 ounces) butter, divided
½–¾ cup flour
½ gallon milk
1 pound fresh mushrooms, sliced
1½ cups onions, chopped
4 cups mayonnaise
12 ounces diced pimentos, drained
3 pounds baked ham, chopped
4–5 pounds Cheddar cheese, shredded
1 pound Ritz™ crackers, crumbled

Preheat oven to 350°F. Cook macaroni according to package directions and drain. In a large pot, melt 1 stick of butter. Gradually add flour, stirring constantly to make a thick paste. Gradually add milk, stirring constantly to prevent lumps. Stir until sauce is thick and smooth. In a separate pan, melt 1 stick butter and lightly sauté mushrooms and onions. In the large pot containing the butter/flour mixture, combine all ingredients except the crackers and remaining 2 sticks of butter. Pour into greased pans. (Can be covered and refrigerated for a day or frozen at this point.) Bake for 45 minutes. Before serving, melt 2 sticks of butter and mix with crumbled crackers. Cover top of macaroni with buttered crumbs.

—Frances, ALABAMA

Thickened Potatoes

This was a staple dish for farm folk who raised potatoes.
We never ate rice but always had potatoes.

Makes 6 Servings

4 cups white potatoes
¼ cup flour
1 cup milk
Salt, to taste
Pepper, to taste

Peel and quarter potatoes. Transfer to pot and cover with water. Boil until potatoes puncture easily with a fork. Drain water from potatoes. Season with salt and pepper. In a small bowl, combine flour and milk; whisk. Add mixture to potatoes and stir to combine. Consistency will be lumpy. Cook uncovered on low heat for 10–15 minutes. Do not boil.

—*David*, MISSISSIPPI

Potato Patties
(See Thickened Potatoes Recipe)

Makes 4 Servings

1½ cups leftover thickened potatoes
2 eggs, beaten
¼ cup flour
¼–½ cup milk
Vegetable oil, for frying

In a bowl, mash potatoes lightly with a fork. Add eggs and flour; stir to combine. Slowly add milk to potatoes. The consistency should be stiffer than pancake batter. Heat oil in pan on medium high heat. Spoon batter into skillet to form patties about 3 inches in diameter. Brown patties on both sides and serve.

—*David*, MISSISSIPPI

Potluck Potatoes

Makes 10 to 12 Servings

5 medium red potatoes, quartered
1 medium onion, thinly sliced
½ stick (¼ cup) butter, melted
Salt, to taste
Pepper, to taste
6–8 slices bacon, cooked crisp and crumbled
½ cup Cheddar cheese, shredded

Preheat oven to 375°F. Place quartered potatoes and onion slices in a large baking dish; coat with melted butter and sprinkle with salt and pepper. Cover with foil and bake for 45 minutes. Remove from oven and sprinkle with cooked, crumbled bacon and cheese. Cover with foil and set aside for 5 minutes or until cheese is melted.

—Ann, TENNESSEE

Garlic Roasted Potatoes

Makes 8 Servings

3 pounds small red potatoes
¼ cup olive oil
6 cloves garlic, minced
2 tablespoons dried rosemary, crushed
¾ teaspoon salt
½ teaspoon pepper

Preheat oven to 400°F. Pierce each potato several times with a fork. Coat each potato with olive oil and place in 9x13x2-inch baking dish. Sprinkle all sides of potatoes with garlic, rosemary, salt, and pepper. Bake for 50 minutes or until potatoes are tender.

—Yvonne, SOUTH CAROLINA

Thai Potato Curry

Makes 6 Servings

2 teaspoons vegetable oil
1 large onion, chopped
2½ teaspoons Thai green curry paste
1 pound red potatoes, cut in ½-inch cubes
⅓ cup coconut milk
½ cup vegetable broth
1 cup canned crushed tomatoes, with juice
1 tablespoon fresh lime juice
1 tablespoon fresh basil, chopped
3 cups cooked rice, for serving

Heat the oil in a wok or large skillet over medium heat. Add the onion and cook until golden, 5–7 minutes. Add the curry paste and stir-fry for 1 minute. Add the potatoes; toss well to coat. Stir in the coconut milk and broth. Add the crushed tomatoes and juice to the potatoes. Cover and simmer until potatoes are tender, about 15–20 minutes. Stir in lime juice and basil. Serve over rice.

—Misty, LOUISIANA

*What I say is that, if a fellow
really likes potatoes, he must be
a pretty decent sort of fellow.*

—A.A. MILNE

Potato Puffs

Makes 4 Servings

2 cups potatoes, cooked and mashed
2 eggs, slightly beaten
1 cup flour
2 teaspoons baking powder
¼ cup cheese, grated (optional)
¼ cup onion, diced (optional)
1 teaspoon salt
¼ teaspoon pepper
Vegetable oil, for frying

In a large bowl, combine all ingredients; mix well. Cover and refrigerate for 1 hour.

Heat oil in a deep-fat fryer. Drop potato mixture by heaping tablespoons into hot oil. Cook until golden brown.

—*Linda and Betty,* NORTH CAROLINA

Unfried French Fries

Makes 6 Servings

2¾ pounds (5 large) baking potatoes
2 egg whites
1 tablespoon Cajun seasoning

Preheat oven to 400°F. Spray baking sheet with non-stick cooking oil. Slice potatoes into matchstick-size pieces. In a large mixing bowl, beat egg whites with Cajun seasoning. Add potatoes and toss to coat. Place coated potato slices on oiled baking sheet in a single layer. Bake for 40–45 minutes, turning to brown evenly.

—*Linda,* NORTH CAROLINA

Praline
Sweet Potato Casserole

Makes 6 Servings

POTATOES:
3 cups sweet potatoes, cooked and mashed
½ cup milk
3 eggs, beaten
1 cup plus 1 tablespoon sugar
1 tablespoon vanilla
1 stick (½ cup) butter, melted

TOPPING:
1 cup brown sugar
½ cup flour
1 cup pecans, chopped
1 stick (½ cup) butter or margarine

Potatoes: Preheat oven to 350°F. Combine all potato ingredients in a large mixing bowl. Beat until mixture is smooth. Pour into a 2-quart baking dish.

Topping: In a separate bowl, mix brown sugar, flour, and pecans. Cut in butter until mixture is crumbly. Sprinkle topping evenly over potato mixture.

Bake for 30 minutes.

—*Sarah,* ALABAMA

Sweet Potato Orange Cups

Makes 16 Servings

5 cups (6–8) sweet potatoes, cooked and mashed

8 oranges, halved, with fruit scooped out,
   and fruit and peel cups reserved

1½ cups brown sugar

¾ cup pecans, chopped, divided

½ cup coconut

½ cup crushed pineapple

½ cup dark raisins

½ teaspoon nutmeg

1 teaspoon cinnamon

Dash of salt

Set aside ½ cup of fruit from orange. Juice remaining fruit from oranges until ½ cup of juice can be reserved. Soak raisins in ½ cup of orange juice until orange flavor is absorbed. Drain.

In large bowl, combine cooked, mashed sweet potatoes, ½ cup of fruit from orange, brown sugar, ½ cup chopped pecans, coconut, crushed pineapple, pre-soaked raisins, nutmeg, cinnamon, and salt. Spoon the sweet potato mixture into the orange cups and sprinkle remaining ¼ cup chopped pecans on top.

—*Nancy,* VIRGINIA

Grandma's Cashew Nut Dressing

Makes 4 Servings

CORNBREAD:

2 cups flour

1 cup white cornmeal

3 teaspoons baking powder

¼ teaspoon baking soda

4 tablespoons shortening

1 egg, beaten

1 teaspoon salt

¾–1 cup buttermilk

DRESSING:

6 eggs, hard-boiled and mashed

Salt, to taste

Pepper, to taste

1 cup celery, diced

8 ounces cashews, halves or pieces

1–2 cups chicken or turkey broth

Cornbread: Preheat oven to 450°. In a large bowl, combine the first 7 cornbread ingredients and mix well. Add enough buttermilk to make a stiff batter. Bake in iron frying pan until golden.

Dressing: In a separate large bowl, break cornbread into bite-size pieces; add mashed eggs, salt, and pepper. Add celery and cashews. Mix with broth until well moistened. Place in Dutch oven, and bake at 350°F until browned.

—*Eugenia,* ALABAMA

Pecan, Rice, and Crawfish Dressing

Makes 12 Servings

1 medium onion, chopped

1 stalk celery, chopped

1 green bell pepper, chopped

1 pound lean ground beef

2 cloves garlic, minced

2 (16-ounce) packages frozen peeled and
   cooked crawfish tails, thawed

2 cups long-grain rice, cooked

1 cup pecans, chopped and toasted

¼ cup butter, cut into pieces

6 green onions, chopped

2 tablespoons Creole seasoning

½ teaspoon pepper

Fresh parsley, chopped, for garnish

Preheat oven to 350°F. In a Dutch oven over medium-high heat, cook first 5 ingredients stirring until beef is brown and crumbly. Stir in crawfish and next 6 ingredients; cook 3 minutes or until heated through. Spoon mixture into a lightly greased 13x9-inch baking dish. Bake for 25–30 minutes or until lightly browned. Sprinkle with parsley.

—*Laura*, MISSISSIPPI

Old-Fashioned Cornbread Dressing

Makes 8 to 10 Servings

CHICKEN AND BROTH:

3–4 pounds chicken, cut up
1–2 quarts of water,
    enough to cover chicken
1 large onion, quartered
3 stalks celery, quartered
4 cloves garlic
1 medium bell pepper,
    quartered

2 carrots, quartered
3 bay leaves
¼ cup fresh parsley
1½ teaspoons pepper
1 teaspoon salt

CORNBREAD:

1 cup white corn flour
½ teaspoon salt
½ teaspoon baking powder
½ teaspoon baking soda

1 egg
6 ounces milk
1 tablespoon vegetable oil

DRESSING:

2 tablespoons butter
1 cup onions, chopped
3 stalks celery, chopped
¼ cup parsley, chopped
2½ cups chicken broth,
    reserved from chicken
    and broth preparation
1 cup milk
2 eggs, beaten

1 teaspoon poultry seasoning
Salt, to taste
Pepper, to taste
Chicken, coarsely chopped,
    reserved from chicken
    and broth preparation
Cornbread, crumbled

Chicken and Broth: Place all chicken and broth ingredients in a large stockpot and bring to a boil. Simmer until chicken is tender. Remove the chicken and set aside to cool. When cool, remove bones from chicken and coarsely chop. Strain broth and discard vegetables. Set chicken and broth aside to use in dressing.

(continued on next page)

Cornbread: Preheat oven to 475°F. Grease a black iron skillet and preheat skillet in the oven. In a medium bowl, whisk flour, salt, baking powder, and baking soda. In a separate bowl, beat egg; add milk and vegetable oil; mix well. Add the wet ingredients to the dry ingredients; stir to combine. Pour batter into the preheated skillet. Bake 15–20 minutes until golden brown. Set aside to use in dressing.

Dressing: Preheat oven to 450°F. In a skillet, melt butter; add chopped onions, celery, and parsley. Sauté until onions are tender. In a large bowl, combine remaining ingredients. You may want to use more or less of the broth for a more or less moist dressing. Spoon dressing into a lightly greased baking pan. Bake for 25-30 minutes.

—*Marie,* MISSISSIPPI

" *Laughter is brightest,*
in the place where food is. "

—IRISH PROVERB

Oyster Dressing

Makes 10 Servings

1 pint (2½ cups) oysters, fresh or frozen
½ cup butter
1 cup onions, finely chopped
½ cup celery, chopped
¼ cup parsley, chopped
1 (8-ounce) package cornbread stuffing mix
1 egg, beaten
1 (8-ounce) can sliced water chestnuts, drained
1 teaspoon salt
½ teaspoon thyme
½ teaspoon sage
¼ teaspoon pepper

Preheat oven to 350°F if dressing will be baked in a pan in the oven. If stuffing will be cooked inside the bird, follow the directions for the turkey to be stuffed, and preheat the oven accordingly. Thaw oysters, if frozen. Drain oysters, reserving liquid. Remove and discard any remaining shell particles. Set oysters aside. Melt butter in a small frying pan. Sauté onion, celery, and parsley in the butter until tender, but not brown. Pour reserved oyster liquid into a measuring cup and add water until total liquid equals 1 cup. In a large bowl, combine stuffing mix, egg, and water/oyster liquid. Toss lightly to blend. Add vegetable mixture, oysters, water chestnuts, and seasonings to stuffing mixture in bowl; stir to combine. Spoon dressing loosely into cavity of 10–12 pound turkey. Bake according to turkey directions. Stuffing may also be baked in a lightly greased 2-quart baking dish for 15–20 minutes.

—*Nancy,* SOUTH CAROLINA

Breads and More

> *Eating well gives
> a spectacular joy to life.*
>
> —ELSA SCHIAPARELLI

Easy Potato Rolls

Makes 45 Rolls

2 packages (4½ teaspoons) dry active yeast
1⅓ cup water, warmed to 110°F–115°F, divided
⅔ cup sugar
⅔ cup shortening
1 cup potatoes, cooked and mashed
2½ teaspoons salt
2 eggs, beaten
6–6½ cups flour

In a small bowl, dissolve yeast in ⅔ cup of the warm water. Set aside. In a large bowl, cream sugar and shortening. Add potatoes, salt, beaten eggs, and dissolved yeast. Stir to combine. Beat in 2 cups flour and remaining ⅔ cup of warm water. Continue to add flour until batter forms a soft dough. Shape dough into a ball; do not knead. Place dough into a large, greased bowl, turning once to coat surface of dough with grease. Cover and let rise in a warm place until doubled in size, about 1 hour.

Grease 3 baking sheets. Punch dough down and divide into three equal portions. Divide each portion into 15 balls. Arrange balls on baking sheets. Do not crowd. Cover and let rise until dough has doubled in bulk, about 30 minutes.

Preheat oven to 375°F. Bake rolls for 20–25 minutes. Remove from pans and cool on wire racks.

—*Nancy,* ALABAMA

Mother's Wonderful Rolls

Sinfully delicious!

Makes 36 Rolls

2 packages (4½ teaspoons) dry yeast
1 cup plus 1 tablespoon sugar
¼ cup lukewarm water
1 cup milk
1 stick (½ cup) butter, room temperature
5 cups flour, sifted and divided
1½ teaspoons salt
3 large eggs, well beaten
½ stick (¼ cup) butter, melted

In a small bowl, dissolve yeast and 1 tablespoon of sugar in lukewarm water. Set aside. In a large bowl, combine milk, ½ cup room temperature butter, and 1 cup of sugar. Beat until sugar is dissolved. Add yeast mixture, 3 cups flour, and salt. Stir until well blended. Add the eggs and 2 cups of flour. Mix well. Let rise until dough has doubled in size.

Roll out on a floured surface until dough is ⅓-inch thick. Brush top of dough with melted butter. Fold dough in half with buttered surface in the middle. Cut into desired shapes and place on baking sheets. Let rise for 1 hour.

Preheat oven to 400°F. Bake for 10 minutes or until rolls are golden brown. Cool on a wire rack.

—*Mari*, ARKANSAS

Angel Biscuits

These are more like easy yeast rolls than biscuits!

Makes 24 Biscuits

1 package (2¼ teaspoons) active dry yeast
2 tablespoons warm water
5 cups flour
1 teaspoon baking soda
3 teaspoons baking powder
1½ teaspoons salt
2 tablespoons sugar
1 cup shortening
2 cups buttermilk

In a small bowl, dissolve yeast in 2 tablespoons of warm water. Set aside. Sift flour, baking soda, baking powder, salt, and sugar into a large bowl. Cut in shortening until mixture resembles coarse crumbs. Add buttermilk and dissolved yeast to the dry ingredients. Mix well. Cover and refrigerate overnight or for up to a week.

Preheat oven to 400°F. Generously flour a flat surface. Place dough on floured surface and pat gently until ⅓-inch thick. Fold dough in half. Dough will be sticky, so keep your hands greased and floured. Using a biscuit cutter, shape into rounds. Place the biscuits on ungreased baking sheets, cover, and allow dough to rise for about 45 minutes. Bake for 12–15 minutes or until golden brown.

—*Mary Lou,* ALABAMA

Blueberry Biscuits

Makes 12 Biscuits

BISCUITS:
2 cups flour
2 teaspoons baking powder
¼ teaspoon baking soda
1 teaspoon salt
½ cup sugar
⅓ cup shortening
1 large egg
¾ cup buttermilk
⅓ cup fresh blueberries

TOPPING:
3 tablespoons butter, melted
2 tablespoons sugar
¼ teaspoon cinnamon

Biscuits: Preheat oven to 400°F. In a large bowl, combine flour, baking powder, baking soda, salt, and sugar. Using a pastry blender or two butter knives, cut in shortening. Mixture should resemble coarse crumbs. In a separate bowl, whisk egg and buttermilk. Add wet ingredients to flour mixture and stir just until dry ingredients are moistened. Gently fold in blueberries. Place dough on a lightly floured surface. Pat or roll dough until it is ¾-inch thick. Use a 2¾-inch round cutter to shape into rounds. Arrange biscuits on a lightly greased baking sheet and bake for 15 minutes or until golden brown.

Topping: Melt butter in a small saucepan. Remove from heat and stir in the sugar and cinnamon.

Allow baked biscuits to cool slightly. Brush topping over the warm biscuits.

—*Laura,* MISSISSIPPI

Fluffy Biscuits

Makes 12 Biscuits

2 cups flour
4 teaspoons baking powder
3 teaspoons sugar
½ teaspoon salt
½ cup shortening
1 egg
²/₃ cup milk

Preheat oven to 450°F. In a large bowl, mix flour, baking powder, sugar, and salt. Cut in shortening until the dough resembles coarse crumbs. In a separate bowl, beat egg with milk and stir into flour mixture until just moistened. Knead 20 times. Transfer dough to a flat and lightly floured surface. Roll out dough until ¾-inch thick. Cut into biscuits and place on a greased baking sheet. Bake for 8–10 minutes or until tops are golden brown.

—*Trenda,* KENTUCKY

Lemon Thyme Cream Biscuits

Makes 6 Biscuits

2 teaspoons fresh lemon thyme, minced
2 cups flour
3 tablespoons sugar
1 tablespoon baking powder
½ teaspoon kosher salt
1 ¼ cup heavy cream

Preheat oven to 425°F. Lightly grease or line a baking sheet with parchment paper. In a large bowl, mix lemon thyme, flour, sugar, baking powder, and salt. Gently stir in cream until dry ingredients are just moistened. Place the dough on a lightly floured surface and knead gently just until dough holds together. Add more cream if necessary. Roll or pat dough into a ¾-inch thick circle. Cut into 2- or 3-inch rounds using a biscuit cutter. Arrange biscuits on baking sheet. Do not crowd. Bake biscuits for 15 minutes, or until lightly browned. Serve immediately or transfer to a wire rack to cool.

—*Kim,* SOUTH CAROLINA

Southern Biscuits

Makes 6 Biscuits

1 cup plus 2 tablespoons flour
1 teaspoon baking powder
½ teaspoon salt
¼ teaspoon baking soda
2 tablespoons vegetable shortening
    or butter, plus more for frying
½ cup buttermilk

Preheat oven to 450°F. In a large bowl, combine the dry ingredients. Use two butter knives or a pastry blender to cut in the 2 tablespoons shortening or butter. The mixture should resemble coarse crumbs. Add the buttermilk and use a fork to mix ingredients until just combined. Do not over-mix. Place the dough on a floured surface. Gently pat the dough until it is ½-inch thick. Do not handle the dough too much or it will get tough. Cut into circles using a biscuit cutter.

Place 1 tablespoon vegetable shortening in a heavy iron frying pan and place the pan in the oven for about 7 minutes. Remove the pan from the oven and transfer the biscuits to the pan. Return pan to oven and bake 10–12 minutes, turning once to coat both sides of biscuit with the melted shortening. Biscuits will be golden brown when baked.

—*Sheba*, GEORGIA

Virginia Spoonbread

Makes 4 Servings

*This is not a "pick-up" bread.
It is served with a spoon and eaten with a fork.*

1 cup milk
½ cup cornmeal
½ teaspoon salt
1 egg, separated
1 teaspoon baking powder

Preheat oven to 450°F. Grease an 8x4-inch loaf pan and place it in the oven to heat. In a medium bowl, whisk the egg white until it forms stiff peaks. Set aside. In a medium saucepan, add milk and bring to a boil. Remove from heat and stir in cornmeal. Let cool until lukewarm. Add salt, egg yolk, baking powder, and egg white. Stir until combined. Pour into hot baking dish. Bake for 15 minutes and serve immediately.

—*Allie Mae*, ARKANSAS

*When you are feeling sick …
you want loving care and comfort.
The foods that fill that need are simple,
easy to eat, and cooked with love.*

—JOYCE GOLDSTEIN

Mama's Coush Coush

Sure to warm your innards on a cold morning.
This is the way my mom made it.

Makes 4 Servings

2 cups yellow cornmeal
1 cup flour
2 teaspoons salt
4 teaspoons sugar
2 teaspoons baking powder
1 cup milk
1 egg, beaten
¾ cup cooking oil, divided
Warm milk, for serving
Sugar, for serving

In a large bowl, combine dry ingredients. In a small bowl, mix the milk, egg, and ¼ cup of oil; add to dry ingredients. Pour ½ cup of oil in a heavy pot; heat until very hot. Pour batter into pot. Allow a crust to form before stirring. When a crust has formed, stir until cooked and crunchy; will be lumpy. Serve with warm milk and a pinch of sugar.

—*Jackie*, LOUISIANA

Great Grandma's Cornbread

Makes 1 Loaf

1 cup cornmeal
1 tablespoon baking powder
1 tablespoon sugar
1 cup flour
½ teaspoon salt
1 egg, beaten
⅔ cup buttermilk
2 tablespoons bacon grease

Preheat oven to 400°F. Grease a 9x13-inch baking pan. In a large bowl, combine cornmeal, baking powder, sugar, flour, and salt. Stir and set aside. In a small bowl, add egg and buttermilk; mix well. Cut the bacon grease into dry ingredients. Add wet ingredients to the dry ingredients and stir to combine. Pour into greased baking dish and bake for 20–25 minutes or until top is golden brown.

—*Mary,* ARKANSAS

Cracklin' Bread

Makes 6 Servings

1 cup cracklin's
2 cups cornmeal
1 teaspoon baking powder
⅛ teaspoon salt
1 cup buttermilk

Grease and heat iron skillet to 425°F. In a mixing bowl, combine cracklin's, cornmeal, baking powder, baking soda, and salt. Stir in buttermilk; mix well. Pour batter into skillet. Bake for 20–25 minutes.

—*Linda,* ALABAMA

Sausage Bread

Makes 2 Loaves

2 cups flour
1 teaspoon baking soda
2 teaspoons baking powder
½ teaspoon salt
¼ teaspoon cloves
1 teaspoon cinnamon
½ teaspoon nutmeg
1 egg, lightly beaten
3 cups brown sugar
1 cup strong coffee, cold
2 teaspoons vanilla
1 pound ground mild sausage, browned and drained
¼ cup raisins
½ cup nuts, coarsely chopped

Preheat oven to 350°F. Lightly grease 2 (8x4-inch) loaf pans.
In a large bowl, sift flour, baking soda, baking powder, salt, cloves,
cinnamon, and nutmeg. Stir in egg, brown sugar, coffee, and
vanilla. Add browned and drained sausage, raisins, and nuts.
Mix gently. Pour into pans. Bake for 1½ hours or until a toothpick
inserted in the center comes out clean.

—*Linda,* SOUTH CAROLINA

Sweet Potato Bread

Makes 2 Loaves

3 medium (2 cups) sweet potatoes, grated
1 whole egg
2 egg whites
1 cup light brown sugar or honey
¾ cup canola oil
3 cups flour
1 teaspoon salt
1 teaspoon baking soda
¼ teaspoon baking powder
1½ teaspoons cinnamon
¼ teaspoon nutmeg
2 medium (1 cup) bananas, mashed
½ cup pecans, chopped (optional)
1 cup raisins

Preheat oven to 350°F. Grease 2 (8x4-inch) loaf pans. In a large bowl, combine sweet potatoes, egg, egg whites, and sugar or honey. Add oil and mix well. In a separate bowl, sift flour and combine with salt, baking soda, baking powder, cinnamon, and nutmeg. Add dry ingredients to wet ingredients. Stir in bananas, pecans if desired, and raisins. Divide batter evenly between pans. Bake for 1 hour, or until a toothpick inserted in the center comes out clean.

—*Don,* LOUISIANA

Sour Cream Pecan Bread

Makes 3 Loaves   **For a Crowd**

2½ cups sugar

1½ cups butter, divided

5 eggs, divided

4 cups plus 1½ tablespoons unbleached flour, divided

1½ teaspoons salt

½ teaspoon baking powder

½ teaspoon baking soda

1½ cups light sour cream

1 pound (4 cups) pecans, chopped, divided

1½ teaspoons vanilla

1½ cups brown sugar

1 teaspoon cinnamon

Preheat oven to 350°F. Grease 3 (9x5-inch) loaf pans and set aside. In a large mixing bowl, cream sugar and 1 cup butter. Using an electric mixer, beat in 3 eggs. Sift 2 cups flour, salt, baking powder, and baking soda into a separate bowl. Add dry mixture to the egg mixture. Beat in remaining 2 eggs. Add 2 more cups of flour and blend. Stir in sour cream, 2 cups of pecans, and vanilla. Pour into prepared loaf pans. In a large bowl, combine brown sugar, ½ cup butter, 1½ tablespoons flour, cinnamon, and 2 cups of pecans. Mix well. Sprinkle mixture over loaves and pat mixture lightly to assure adherence to the top of bread. Bake 1 hour and 25 minutes or until a toothpick inserted in the center comes out clean. If the tops of loaves are browning too quickly, loosely cover pans with a tent of aluminum foil. Cool in pans for 5 minutes. Transfer to wire racks and cool completely before slicing.

—*Robin*, KENTUCKY

Bishops Bread

Makes 1 Loaf

BREAD:
½ cup soft-spread margarine
¾ cup sugar
1 teaspoon vanilla
2 eggs
2¾ cups flour, sifted
3 teaspoons baking powder
½ teaspoon salt
1 cup milk
$\frac{1}{3}$ cup nuts, finely chopped
$\frac{1}{3}$ cup candied cherries
$\frac{1}{3}$ cup semisweet chocolate chips
$\frac{1}{3}$ cup raisins

FROSTING:
2 tablespoons soft-spread margarine
1½ cups powdered sugar, sifted

Bread: Preheat oven to 350°F. Grease a 9x5-inch loaf pan. In a large bowl, cream margarine, sugar, and vanilla. Beat in eggs one at a time. Sift flour, baking powder, and salt into a separate bowl. Alternate additions of ½ cup of dry ingredients and a little milk to the butter mixture until dry ingredients and milk are combined. Stir in nuts, cherries, chocolate chips, and raisins. Pour into loaf pan. Bake for 1 hour and 5 minutes or until a toothpick inserted in the center comes out clean.

Frosting: In a small bowl, cream margarine and sifted powdered sugar.

Spread frosting over the bread.

—*Sue*, LOUISIANA

Cranberry Coffee Cake

Makes 1 Large Coffee Cake

COFFEE CAKE:
2 cups self-rising flour
1 cup sugar
2 eggs, beaten
1 cup sour cream
1 (16-ounce) can whole berry cranberry sauce

TOPPING:
3 tablespoons flour
$^1/_3$ cup brown sugar
1 teaspoon cinnamon
2 teaspoons butter, softened

Coffee Cake: Preheat oven to 350°F. Grease a 9x13x2-inch baking pan. In a large bowl, combine flour and sugar. In a separate bowl, blend eggs and sour cream; add to flour mixture. Stir until smooth. Pour half of the batter into the baking dish. Cover with cranberry sauce. Top with the remaining batter.

Topping: In a medium bowl, mix flour, brown sugar, and cinnamon. Cut in butter until topping resembles coarse crumbs.

Sprinkle coffee cake with topping. Bake until golden brown, 30–40 minutes.

—*Sally,* VIRGINIA

Luscious Butter Coffee Cake

Makes 1 Coffee Cake

COFFEE CAKE:
2 teaspoons baking soda, divided
1 cup sour cream
1½ cups flour, sifted
½ cup butter
1 cup sugar
2 eggs, lightly beaten
1½ teaspoons vanilla

TOPPING:
½ cup sugar
1 teaspoon cinnamon
¼ cup walnuts, chopped

Coffee Cake: Preheat oven to 350°F. In a small bowl, add ½ teaspoon of the baking soda to the sour cream and let stand for 10 minutes. Grease a 9x13-inch baking pan; set aside. Sift flour and 1½ teaspoons of the baking soda into a medium bowl; set aside. In a large bowl, cream butter and sugar. Alternate additions of the flour mixture, sour cream, and beaten eggs to the butter mixture, beating well after each addition. Stir in vanilla.

Topping: In a medium bowl, mix sugar, cinnamon, and walnuts.

Pour half of the batter into the baking pan. Spoon half of the topping over the batter. Add the remaining batter and sprinkle with the rest of the topping. Bake for 45 minutes or until a toothpick inserted in the center comes out clean.

—*Lettie,* VIRGINIA

Morning Glory Muffins

Makes 18 Muffins

2 cups flour
2 teaspoons baking soda
2 teaspoons cinnamon
½ teaspoon salt
1 cup sugar
3 eggs, lightly beaten
1 cup vegetable oil
1 teaspoon vanilla
1 cup pecans, chopped
1 cup raisins
1 cup coconut
1 cup carrots, grated
1 cup apple, grated

Preheat oven to 300°F. Line 18 muffin cups with paper liners.
In a large bowl, mix flour, baking soda, cinnamon, salt, and sugar.
Stir in eggs, oil, and vanilla. Add all remaining ingredients and mix
thoroughly. Spoon batter into muffin cups. Bake for 15–20 minutes.

—*Charmein*, ALABAMA

"
*Food and charity
make a wonderful blend.*
—PAUL NEWMAN
"

Glazed Cinnamon Raisin Rolls

Makes 12 Cinnamon Rolls

ROLLS:

3½ cups flour, divided
1 package (2¼ teaspoons) yeast
1¼ cups milk
¼ cup sugar

¼ cup shortening
1 teaspoon salt
1 egg

FILLING:

½ cup sugar
¼ cup butter, melted

2 teaspoons cinnamon
½ cup raisins

GLAZE:

1 cup powdered sugar, sifted
1–2 tablespoons milk

½ teaspoon vanilla

Rolls: In a large bowl, combine 2 cups flour and the yeast. Stir and set aside. In a saucepan, heat milk, sugar, shortening, and salt over medium heat. When the temperature measures 120°F on an instant-read thermometer, pour the milk mixture into the yeast mixture. Add the egg and beat with an electric mixer on low speed for 30 seconds. Then beat on high speed for 3 minutes. Stir in the remaining 1½ cups flour. Form dough into a ball and place the dough in a deep greased bowl. Cover and let rise in a warm place until doubled in size, about 1½–2 hours. When dough has doubled, transfer to a floured work surface; do not punch down. Roll out or press dough gently into a 16x10-inch rectangle.

Filling: In a medium bowl, combine all filling ingredients and mix well. Sprinkle the filling over the dough.

Starting at the long side of the dough rectangle, tightly roll dough. Pinch seam and ends to seal. Cut into 12 equal slices. Place on greased baking sheets. Cover. Let rise until dough has doubled, about 1 hour. Preheat oven to 325°F. Uncover rolls and bake for 35 minutes or until tops are golden brown.

Glaze: In a medium bowl, combine all glaze ingredients. Stir until the glaze is smooth. Pour glaze over the warm rolls.

—*Nancy,* ALABAMA

Raised Doughnuts

Makes 15 Doughnuts

1 (0.6-ounce) package cake yeast, crumbled
½ cup lukewarm water
4½ cups flour, sifted and divided
½ cup plus 1½ teaspoons sugar
½ cup shortening, plus more for frying
½ teaspoon salt
2 eggs, beaten
1 teaspoon vanilla
½ cup milk
Powdered sugar, for dusting

Dissolve yeast in ½ cup lukewarm water. In a warm mixing bowl, combine ½ cup of flour and 1½ teaspoons of sugar. Add dissolved yeast to flour/sugar mixture and stir until well blended. Cover and let dough rise in a warm place for 20 minutes. In a separate bowl, cream shortening and the remaining ½ cup sugar. Add salt, eggs, vanilla, and milk. Stir in as much of the remaining flour as you can without getting your spoon stuck. Add the yeast mixture and knead the rest of the flour into the dough. Cover dough and let rise for 3–4 hours or until it has doubled in size. Place dough on a floured surface and pat gently until ½-inch thick. Cut dough into rings with a doughnut cutter. Place rings on a floured surface and let rise until doughnuts have doubled in size.

In a large frying pan, add shortening and heat to 385°F. Fry each doughnut 1½–2 minutes on each side until browned, turning only once. You can fry several doughnuts at a time, but don't crowd them. Drain on paper towels. Dust with powdered sugar while doughnuts are still warm.

—*Roy*, NORTH CAROLINA

Beignets

Makes 8 to 10 Beignets

2 packages (4½ teaspoons) yeast
4 tablespoons plus ⅛ teaspoon sugar
¾ cup lukewarm water
2 cups lukewarm milk
¼ teaspoon salt
2 eggs
3¼ cups oil, divided
6 cups flour
Powdered sugar, for baking sheet and dusting beignets

In a medium bowl, dissolve yeast and ⅛ teaspoon sugar in lukewarm water. Set aside and allow yeast to rise until doubled in size. In a large bowl, mix lukewarm milk, 4 tablespoons sugar, salt, eggs, and ¼ cup oil. When yeast has doubled in size, add to milk mixture. Stir in flour 1 cup at a time. Add enough flour so that dough can be handled. Flour a smooth work surface and knead dough until flexible. The dough should bounce back if you stick a finger in it. Place dough in a deep oiled bowl and cover it with a towel. Set in a warm place and let rise 45 minutes or until dough has doubled in size.

Heat 3 cups of oil in a Dutch oven to 350°F. Divide dough into 4 equal portions. Roll out each portion of dough on floured surface until ⅛-inch thick. Cut into 2½x3-inch triangles or squares. Drop dough, piece by piece, into hot oil. Do not crowd. Turn each beignet once, to brown both sides. Remove from oil. Drain on paper towels. Cover the bottom of a cookie sheet with a light coating of powdered sugar. Place fried beignets on the cookie sheet and sprinkle the tops with additional powdered sugar. A small wire sieve works great for dusting the tops of the beignets.

—*Don*, LOUISIANA

Tar Heel Hushpuppies

Makes 24 Hushpuppies

1 quart of peanut oil, for frying
2 cups white cornmeal
1 tablespoon flour
2 teaspoons sugar
½ teaspoon baking soda
1 teaspoon baking powder
1½ teaspoons salt
1 cup buttermilk
1 small onion, finely chopped
1 egg, beaten

Pour oil into a deep fryer and preheat to 375°F. In a large bowl, combine remaining ingredients, adding the beaten egg last; mix well. Drop one tablespoon of batter at a time into the hot oil. In about 3 minutes, hushpuppies will be golden brown and will float to the top of the oil. Use a slotted spoon or tongs to remove hush-puppies from the oil. Drain on absorbent paper towels. Serve warm.

—*Mare*, VIRGINIA

It's a fine spring evening in the South.

Fresh-caught fish coated with seasoned cornmeal are frying in a pan over an open fire. Fellow parishioners, neighbors, and friends are gathered. Stories are shared. Laughter resonates from the shaded areas beneath the numerous trees. Frisky puppies play. The older dogs lie quietly and loyally by their owner's sides. In part, this idyllic setting is made possible by the introduction of "hushpuppies" early in the twentieth century. One day, a clever individual mixed the cornmeal for the fish with a little milk or water, fried the batter and threw the resulting dumplings to the dogs whining to be fed during the fish fry. The puppies were hushed. This worked so well that seasonings were added, recipes perfected, and today, a Southern fried supper is incomplete without the accompaniment of hushpuppies.

Henry's Cajun-Style Hushpuppies

Makes 24 Hushpuppies

Vegetable oil, for frying
1 cup cornmeal
½ cup flour
2 teaspoons baking powder
½ teaspoon salt
½ teaspoon black pepper
1 teaspoon garlic powder
½ teaspoon paprika
1 teaspoon lemon juice
1 medium onion, finely chopped
1 small green bell pepper, finely chopped
2 jalapeño peppers, finely chopped
1 (8-ounce) can creamed corn
1 egg, beaten

Heat oil in a deep fryer to 375°F. In a large bowl, mix cornmeal, flour, baking powder, salt, black pepper, garlic powder, and paprika. Stir in lemon juice, onion, green pepper, jalapeño peppers, corn, and egg. Batter should have a smooth, thick texture. If mixture is too thick, add water. Drop batter by tablespoonfuls into deep fryer. Fry until golden brown.

—*Henry*, MISSISSIPPI

Ham and Corn Fritters

Makes 18 Fritters

½ cup ground ham, cooked
1 (14-ounce) can whole kernel corn
1 tablespoon grated onion
⅔ cup flour
1½ teaspoons baking powder
½ cup milk
Vegetable oil, for frying

In a bowl, mix cooked ham, corn, and onion. In a separate bowl, sift flour and baking powder. Add dry ingredients to ham mixture; stir to combine. Add milk and mix well. Drop by spoonfuls into deep, hot fat. Fry until golden brown. Drain. Serve warm.

—*Pat and Linda,* NORTH CAROLINA

Cornbread Dumplings

*My Aunt Lulu cooked these dumplings on top of
mustard, collard, or turnip greens.*

Makes 4 Servings

¾ cup flour
½ cup yellow or white cornmeal
1½ teaspoons baking powder
½ teaspoon salt
½ cup milk
2 tablespoons shortening, melted

Sift flour, cornmeal, baking powder, and salt into a large bowl. Stir in milk and melted shortening until all ingredients are moistened. Drop by heaping tablespoonfuls into a pot of boiling greens or soup. Cover pot and boil for 15–20 minutes. Make sure that you add the dumplings 15–20 minutes before the greens are ready to eat.

—*Dorothea,* LOUISIANA

Quick and Easy Pizza Dough

Makes 2 10-inch Pizza Crusts

3 tablespoons olive oil, divided
¾ cup warm (120°F) water
2 cups flour
½ teaspoon salt
½ teaspoon sugar
1 (2¼ teaspoons) package instant yeast
2 tablespoons cornmeal

In a small bowl, add 1 tablespoon of the olive oil to warm water. Set aside. In a large bowl, add flour, salt, sugar, and yeast; stir to combine. Make a well in the center of the dry ingredients and pour the oil/water mixture into the well. Stir until dough forms a ball. Place dough on a lightly floured work surface and knead until smooth, about 10 minutes. Use remaining olive oil to grease a deep bowl. Place dough in bowl and turn to coat surface of dough with the oil. Cover and let dough rise with a warm place for 30–40 minutes.

At least 45 minutes before baking pizzas, put baking stone or baking sheet on bottom rack of oven. Preheat oven to 500°F. Punch down dough and divide into 2 equal portions. Roll each piece into a 10-inch circle. Dust a baker's peel or rimless baking sheet with cornmeal and place one pizza round on dusted surface. Cover with desired toppings. Carefully transfer pizza onto baking stone or baking sheet. Bake until crust is crisp and golden, 8–10 minutes. Repeat with the second crust.

—*Jill*, ALABAMA

Cajun Bagel Chips

Perfect for holiday gift giving

Makes 60 Chips

6 plain bagels, not sliced
½ cup butter, melted
¼ teaspoon dried thyme, crushed
¼ teaspoon onion salt
½ teaspoon ground cayenne pepper
¼ teaspoon black pepper
$^1/_8$ teaspoon garlic powder

Preheat oven to 400°F. Cut bagels vertically into ⅛-inch thick slices, about ten slices per bagel. Set aside. In a small bowl, add melted butter, thyme, onion salt, cayenne pepper, black pepper, and garlic powder; stir to combine. Brush one side of each bagel slice with the butter mixture. Arrange slices on a baking sheet in a single layer. Bake for 5–6 minutes or until top edges of bagel strips are crisp. Turn chips over. Bake 4–5 minutes longer or until crisp. Cool on wire rack.

—*Don*, LOUISIANA

Desserts

> "One of the goldenest
> of the golden rules
> in making up a menu ...
> is to pay special attention
> to the dessert course ...
> nobody seems able to resist
> a delicious dessert."
>
> —WOLFGANG PUCK

Fresh Coconut Cake

Makes 1 Cake

*For a really coconut-y cake, substitute ½ cup of the buttermilk
in the cake batter with ½ cup coconut milk.*

CAKE:

2 cups flour	1 cup buttermilk
1 teaspoon baking soda	1 teaspoon vanilla
1 cup butter	5 egg whites,
2 cups sugar	beaten to stiff peaks
5 egg yolks	

ICING:

1 fresh whole coconut, grated	1 cup coconut milk
and divided with milk reserved	2 tablespoons cornstarch
2 cups sugar	

Cake: Preheat oven to 350°F and line the bottoms of three lightly greased 8-inch round cake pans with parchment paper. In a medium bowl, sift flour with baking soda. Set aside. In a large bowl, cream butter and sugar using an electric mixer at medium speed. Add egg yolks one at a time. Mix in buttermilk and vanilla. Gradually add dry ingredients to the creamy mixture and continue to mix at medium speed until well combined. Gently fold in beaten egg whites. Pour immediately into cake pans and bake 30–40 minutes until a toothpick inserted in the center comes out clean. Place pans on wire racks and cool 5 minutes. Remove from pans; allow cake to cool fully on racks before icing.

Icing: Set 1 cup of grated coconut aside. In a medium saucepan, mix remaining coconut with the sugar, coconut milk, and cornstarch. Cook over medium heat 5–7 minutes until mixture is thick. Allow icing to cool slightly. Spread the icing between cake layers; stack layers. Spread the icing over the top and sides of the cake. Sprinkle the remaining coconut on top.

—*Suzy*, NORTH CAROLINA

Robert E. Lee Cake

Makes 1 Cake

CAKE:

9 egg yolks

2⅛ cups sugar

½ teaspoon salt

1 tablespoon lemon juice,
   freshly squeezed

9 egg whites,
   beaten to stiff peaks

2 cups flour, sifted

FILLING:

3 lemons

6 oranges

3 cups sugar

1 cup coconut, shredded

GARNISH:

Shredded coconut,
Orange slices

Mint leaves or flower blossoms

Cake: Preheat oven to 325°F. In a large bowl, lightly beat the egg yolks. Slowly stir the sugar in with the yolks. Add salt and lemon juice; mix well. Carefully fold in beaten egg whites. Fold in flour. Pour into 3 ungreased 9-inch baking pans. Bake for 25–30 minutes. Place on wire racks to cool.

Filling: In a large bowl, zest the oranges and lemons. Squeeze juice and pulp from the lemons and oranges over the zest in the bowl. Add sugar and coconut; stir well. Let stand until sugar dissolves, stirring occasionally.

Spread the filling between the cake layers and on the top and sides of the cake. Let cake stand for 1 to 2 days to allow the juices to soak into the cake.

Before serving, sprinkle top of cake with shredded coconut. Garnish with orange slices and mint leaves or flower blossoms.

—*Mimi*, NORTH CAROLINA

Sweet Potato Layer Cake

For a Crowd

Makes 3 Cakes

CAKES:

1½ cups vegetable oil	2½ cups flour
2 cups sugar	3 teaspoons baking powder
4 eggs, separated	1 teaspoon ground cinnamon
1½ cups sweet potatoes, uncooked, finely shredded	1 teaspoon ground nutmeg
	¼ teaspoon salt
¼ cup hot water	1 cup pecans, chopped
1 teaspoon vanilla	

FROSTING:

½ cup butter	2⅔ cups flaked coconut
1⅓ cups sugar	1 cup pecans, chopped
2 (5-ounce) cans evaporated milk	2 teaspoons vanilla
4 egg yolks, beaten	

Cakes: Preheat oven to 350°F. Grease 3 (9-inch) round cake pans. In a very large bowl, beat oil and sugar. Add egg yolks, one at a time, beating well after each addition. Add sweet potatoes, water, and vanilla; mix well. In a small bowl, beat egg whites until stiff; fold into sweet potato mixture. In a separate bowl, combine flour, baking powder, cinnamon, nutmeg, and salt; add to potato mixture. Stir in pecans. Divide batter evenly between cake pans. Bake for 22–27 minutes or until toothpick inserted in center comes out clean. Cool. Remove cakes from pans.

Frosting: Melt butter in a saucepan. In a medium bowl, add sugar, milk, and egg yolks; whisk until smooth. Gradually pour melted butter into milk mixture, stirring constantly. Transfer mixture to the saucepan. Cook over medium heat for 10–12 minutes, stirring often until thickened and bubbly. Remove from heat. Stir in coconut, pecans, and vanilla. Allow frosting to cool slightly before spreading on the cake.

Spread a portion of the frosting between each layer of cake. Use the remaining frosting to cover the top and sides of the cakes.

—*Mary,* ALABAMA

Mississippi Mud Cake

Like a Brownie

Makes 1 Cake

CAKE:

¾ cup butter, softened

1½ cups sugar

1½ teaspoons vanilla

3 egg yolks

½ cup plus

   1 tablespoon cocoa powder

½ cup flour

3 tablespoons vegetable oil

3 tablespoons water

¾ cup pecans, finely chopped

3 egg whites, room temperature

$\frac{1}{8}$ teaspoon cream of tartar

$\frac{1}{8}$ teaspoon salt

HOT FUDGE SAUCE:

¾ cup sugar

½ cup cocoa powder

$\frac{2}{3}$ cup evaporated milk

$\frac{1}{3}$ cup light corn syrup

$\frac{1}{3}$ cup butter

1 teaspoon vanilla

Cake: Preheat oven to 350°F. Line bottom of a 9-inch springform pan with aluminum foil; butter foil and sides of pan; set aside. In a large mixing bowl, cream butter, sugar, and vanilla. Add egg yolks, one at a time, beating well after each addition. Add cocoa, flour, oil, and water; mix well. Stir in chopped pecans. In a separate bowl, beat egg whites, cream of tartar, and salt until stiff peaks form; carefully fold into chocolate mixture. Pour batter into prepared pan. Bake 45 minutes or until top begins to crack slightly. Mud cake will not test done in the center. Cool 1 hour. Cover and chill until firm. Remove sides of pan.

Hot Fudge Sauce: Combine sugar and cocoa powder in a medium saucepan. Add evaporated milk and corn syrup; stir until well blended. Cook over low heat, stirring constantly, until mixture reaches a simmer. Simmer and stir for 1–2 minutes. Remove from heat and stir in butter and vanilla.

Cover cake with hot fudge sauce.

—*Linda*, TENNESSEE

Double Chocolate Praline Fudge Cake

This cake may be frozen, if desired.
Thaw for 4 to 6 hours before serving.

Makes 1 Large Cake

FUDGE CAKE:
1 cup butter
¼ cup cocoa powder
1 cup water
½ cup buttermilk
2 large eggs
1 teaspoon baking soda
1 teaspoon vanilla
2 cups flour
2 cups sugar
½ teaspoon salt

CHOCOLATE GARNISH:
12 ounces semi-sweet chocolate morsels
⅓ cup whipping cream

PRALINE FROSTING:
¼ cup butter, cut into pieces
1 cup light brown sugar, firmly packed
⅓ cup whipping cream
1 cup powdered sugar
1 teaspoon vanilla
1 cup pecans, chopped

Fudge Cake: Preheat oven to 350°F. Coat 3 (8-inch) round cake pans with cooking spray and line with parchment paper; set aside. Cook butter, cocoa, and water in a small saucepan over low heat, stirring constantly, until butter melts and mixture is smooth. Remove from heat and allow to cool. Using an electric mixer or whisk, beat buttermilk, eggs, baking soda, and vanilla at medium

(continued on next page)

speed until smooth. Add butter mixture and beat until blended. In a separate bowl, combine flour, sugar, and salt. Add to buttermilk mixture, beating until blended. Batter will be thin. Pour batter into pans. Bake 22–24 minutes or until set. Place pans on wire racks and cool for 10 minutes. Remove cake from pans and allow to cool completely.

Chocolate Garnish: Microwave chocolate and whipping cream in a tempered glass mixing bowl at medium (50%) power for 2–3 minutes or until chocolate is melted. Whisk until smooth. Cool, whisking often, for about 15–20 minutes or until mixture is thick enough to spread. Spread a ½ cup of garnish between each layer of cake. Spread any remaining garnish on sides of the cake. Chill cake for ½ hour.

Praline Frosting: In a 2-quart saucepan over medium heat, add butter, brown sugar, and whipping cream. Bring to a boil and boil for 1 minute. Remove from heat and whisk the mixture in the saucepan. Add powdered sugar and vanilla. Whisk until smooth. Gently stir in pecans. Continue to stir until frosting begins to thicken and cool. Pour frosting slowly over the center of cake. Spread toward the edges of the cake and allow some frosting to run over the sides. Garnish with whole pecans, if desired.

—*Shannon,* NORTH CAROLINA

> *My favorite word is "chocolate."*
> *It's the most delicious word I know …*
> *the word—if I read it or write it*
> *or say it—tastes just great to me.*
>
> —MAIDA HEATTER

Cajun Sheet Cake

Makes 1 Sheet Cake

CAKE:

2 cups self-rising flour, sifted

2 cups sugar

2 sticks (1 cup) butter

4 tablespoons cocoa powder

1 teaspoon vanilla

1 cup (less 1 tablespoon) water

2 eggs, lightly beaten

1 teaspoon cinnamon

½ cup buttermilk

ICING:

1 stick (½ cup) butter

4 tablespoons cocoa powder

6 tablespoons milk

3¾ cups powdered sugar

1 teaspoon vanilla

1 cup pecans, chopped

Cake: Preheat oven to 375°F. Grease a sheet cake pan. In a large mixing bowl, combine sifted flour with sugar and set aside. In a saucepan, mix butter, cocoa, vanilla, and water; bring to a boil. Carefully pour heated mixture over flour/sugar mixture in the bowl. Stir to combine. Add beaten eggs, cinnamon, and buttermilk. Mix well. Pour batter into the prepared sheet pan. Bake for 35 minutes. Prepare icing 5 minutes before cake is finished baking.

Icing: Combine butter, cocoa, and milk in a medium saucepan. Stir to blend and bring mixture to a boil. Remove pan from heat. Stir in the powdered sugar, vanilla, and pecans until well blended.

Carefully pour hot icing over hot cake. Do not cut cake until completely cooled.

—*Lee,* MISSISSIPPI

Old-Fashioned Stack Cake

Makes 1 Large Cake

CAKE:

¾ cup sugar

¼ cup shortening

1 egg

¼ cup molasses

4 cups flour, divided

1 teaspoon baking powder

¾ teaspoon baking soda

¼ teaspoon nutmeg

¼ teaspoon allspice

½ teaspoon cinnamon

¼ teaspoon salt

½ cup buttermilk

FILLING:

1 pound dried apples

Enough water to cover apples

1 cup sugar

1 cup brown sugar

½ teaspoon allspice

¼ teaspoon ground cloves

Cake: Preheat oven to 350°F. Cream sugar and shortening in a large bowl; add egg and beat well. Stir in molasses. In a separate large bowl, combine 1 cup of the flour, baking powder, baking soda, nutmeg, allspice, cinnamon, and salt. Alternate additions of the flour mixture with the buttermilk to the creamed butter mixture. Continue to add additional flour until dough is soft but not sticky. Transfer dough to a lightly floured surface and divide into 6 equal portions. Rollout each portion into a 9-inch round. Prick each round several times with a fork. Bake layers one at a time on a parchment paper–lined baking sheet until golden, about 10–12 minutes.

Filling: Simmer dried apples and water in a saucepan until apples are tender. Remove from heat. Mash apples and add sugars, allspice, and cloves. Cook for 5 more minutes, stirring constantly so apples do not burn. Allow filling to cool before spreading on cake.

While cake is still warm, spread equal amounts of filling on top of each layer and stack layers one at a time.

—*Thelma June,* ALABAMA

Scotch Cake

Makes 1 Cake

1 cup old-fashioned rolled oats
  (Do not use quick oats.)
1 cup boiling water
1 cup flour
1½ cups brown sugar, packed
1 teaspoon salt
1 teaspoon baking soda
1 teaspoon cream of tartar
1 teaspoon cinnamon
½ teaspoon ground cloves
½ cup butter, softened, or applesauce
2 eggs, lightly beaten
1 cup raisins or chopped dates
1 cup nuts, chopped

In a large bowl, combine oats and boiling water. Set aside and let cool. Preheat oven to 350°F. In a medium bowl, combine flour, sugar, salt, baking soda, cream of tartar, cinnamon, and cloves. Gradually stir mixture into the cooled oats. Stir in butter (or applesauce). Add the eggs. When the batter is well mixed, carefully fold in raisins and nuts. Pour into a greased 9x12-inch baking pan. Bake for 30–35 minutes.

—*Margie*, LOUISIANA

Headquartered in Atlanta, Georgia, the Coca-Cola Company has had Southern roots since the first Coca-Cola was sold as a headache remedy in a drugstore in Atlanta in 1886. The Chinese translation of Coca-Cola is the phonetic quivalent of "kokou kole" meaning "happiness in the mouth." The versatility of this carbonated beverage has been tested in recipes ranging from chicken, soup, and barbeque sauce to muffins, ice cream, and the cake recipe found on the facing page. If you accidentally burn the food you are attempting to cook, Coca-Cola can be boiled in the encrusted pan to remove any evidence of your error. If you insisted on eating your burnt food and nausea results, take one teaspoon of flat coke each hour until the nausea subsides.

Coca-Cola™ Cake

Makes 1 Large Cake

CAKE:

2 cups flour

2 cups sugar

1 teaspoon baking soda

½ cup milk

1 teaspoon vanilla

2 eggs, lightly beaten

1 cup Coca-Cola™

2 tablespoons cocoa powder

2 sticks (1 cup) butter

ICING:

½ cup Coca-Cola™

1 stick (½ cup) butter, chopped into pieces

3 tablespoons cocoa powder

3¾ cups powdered sugar

1 cup pecans, chopped and toasted

Cake: Preheat oven to 350°F. Grease and lightly flour a 13x9x2-inch cake pan. In a large bowl, combine flour, sugar, and baking soda. Add milk, vanilla, and lightly beaten eggs. Mix well. In a saucepan, combine Coca-Cola,™ cocoa, and butter; stir and bring to a boil. Carefully add the boiling Coca-Cola™ mixture to the cake batter; mix well. Pour batter into cake pan and bake 40–45 minutes.

Icing: In a saucepan, add Coca-Cola,™ butter, and cocoa; bring to a boil. Stir in sugar and nuts.

Pour slightly cooled icing over warm cake.

—*Carolyn,* NORTH CAROLINA

South Carolina Peach Cake

Makes a delicious summer dessert.
If you end up with leftovers, have them for breakfast the next day.

Makes 1 Cake

3 eggs, well beaten
1 ½ cups sugar
½ cup vegetable oil
2 cups flour
1 teaspoon salt
1 teaspoon baking soda
1 teaspoon cinnamon
2 cups fresh peaches, sliced
1 cup nuts, chopped
Whipped cream, for serving

Preheat oven to 375°F. Grease and flour a 9x13x2-inch baking pan. In a large bowl, add all ingredients and mix until well combined. Pour batter into prepared baking pan. Bake 30–35 minutes. Serve with whipped cream.

—*Shirley*, VIRGINIA

Cajun Syrup Cake with Lemon Glaze

Makes 1 Cake

CAKE:
1 cup boiling water
2 teaspoons baking soda
1 cup Steen's™ 100% Pure Cane Syrup
    (substitute ¾ cup pure molasses and
    ¼ cup water if 100% pure cane syrup is not available)
1½ cups sugar
¾ cup cooking oil
⅛ teaspoon salt
⅛ teaspoon ginger
½ teaspoon cloves
½ teaspoon cinnamon
2½ cups flour, sifted
2 eggs, beaten

GLAZE:
Zest of 1 lemon
¼ cup lemon juice, freshly squeezed
1½ cups powdered sugar

Cake: Preheat oven to 350°F. Pour boiling water into a large tempered glass mixing bowl. Dissolve the baking soda in the boiling water. Add the rest of the cake ingredients and mix well. Grease a 9x13-inch baking pan. Pour batter into the pan and bake 40–45 minutes or until the cake pulls away from the sides of the pan. As soon as you remove the cake from the oven, use a 2-pronged kitchen fork to pierce the cake all the way to the bottom of the pan at 1½-inch intervals.

Glaze: In a medium bowl, combine zest, lemon juice, and powdered sugar and beat until smooth.

Pour glaze over the hot cake and spread smoothly over surface until absorbed.

—*Don*, LOUISIANA

Scripture Cake

Makes 1 Cake

½ cup butter
¾ cup molasses
2 cups flour
½ teaspoon baking soda
¼ teaspoon cinnamon
¼ teaspoon ground cloves
$1/8$ teaspoon ground ginger
¼ teaspoon salt

3 eggs, beaten
½ cup buttermilk
$1/3$ cup honey
1 cup raisins
1 cup dried figs, chopped
½ cup almonds, chopped
½ cup wine or orange juice

Preheat oven to 325°F. Grease and flour a 9x5x3-inch loaf pan. Cream butter in a large mixing bowl; blend in molasses. In a small bowl, combine flour, baking soda, cinnamon, cloves, ginger, and salt. In a third bowl, mix eggs, buttermilk, and honey. Alternate additions of the egg mixture and the dry ingredients to the creamed butter and molasses. Mix well after each addition. Stir in raisins, figs, and almonds. Pour into prepared loaf pan. Bake for 40 minutes. Cover loosely with foil, and bake an additional 50 minutes. Let cool in pan for 10 minutes. Remove from pan and set on wire rack to cool completely. When cake is cool, brush all sides with wine or orange juice and wrap in aluminum foil. Refrigerate for a day or two before serving.

—*Claire*, NORTH CAROLINA

*Cooking demands attention, patience,
and, above all, a respect for the gifts
of the earth. It is a form of worship,
a way of giving thanks.*

—JUDITH B. JONES

Blackberry Jam Cake

Makes 1 Cake

CAKE:
1½ cups sugar
½ cup shortening
3 eggs
½ cup buttermilk
1 teaspoon baking soda
Dash salt
Dash cinnamon
1½ cups flour
1 cup blackberry jam

FROSTING:
1 (8-ounce) package cream cheese
1 stick (½ cup) butter, room temperature
4 cups powdered sugar
1 teaspoon vanilla

Cake: Preheat oven to 350°F. Cream sugar and shortening in a large bowl. Add eggs and beat well. Add buttermilk, baking soda, salt, cinnamon, and flour; stir well to combine. Gently blend in the jam. Pour batter into 2 lightly greased (9-inch) cake pans. Bake 35 minutes or until a toothpick inserted in the center comes out clean. Allow cake to cool.

Frosting: In a large bowl, blend cream cheese and butter. Add powdered sugar and vanilla. Stir until smooth.

Spread frosting between the layers, on top, and on sides of the cake.

—*Mildred,* ARKANSAS

Hummingbird Cake

Makes 1 Cake

CAKE:

3 cups flour

2 cups sugar

1 teaspoon salt

1 teaspoon cinnamon

1 teaspoon baking soda

3 eggs, beaten

1½ cups vegetable oil

1½ teaspoons vanilla

1 (8-ounce) can crushed pineapple, drained

1 cup pecans, chopped

2 cups bananas, mashed

ICING:

1 (8-ounce) package cream cheese

½ cup butter

4 cups powdered sugar, sifted

1 teaspoon vanilla

1 cup pecans, chopped

Cake: Preheat oven to 350°F. Grease and flour 3 (8-inch) round cake pans. In a large bowl, sift flour with sugar, salt, cinnamon, and baking soda. Add beaten eggs and vegetable oil; stir until ingredients are evenly moist. Do not beat. Stir in vanilla, pineapple, pecans, and bananas. Pour into prepared pans. Bake for 25–30 minutes or until a knife inserted in the center of the cake comes out clean. Cool on wire rack.

Icing: In a medium bowl, beat all ingredients except nuts until smooth. Gently stir in pecans.

When cake is cool, spread icing between layers and on the top and sides of the cake.

—*Tammy,* SOUTH CAROLINA

Old-Fashioned Tea Cakes

Makes 36 Tea Cakes   **For a Crowd**

1½ cups flour

2 teaspoons baking powder

1 cup sugar

2 eggs, lightly beaten

½ cup butter, softened

1 teaspoon vanilla

2 teaspoons nutmeg

Preheat oven to 375°F. In a large bowl, sift flour with baking powder. Set aside. In a medium bowl, add the remaining ingredients and stir until creamy. Add the creamy mixture to the dry ingredients and mix thoroughly. Prepare a lightly floured surface and roll out dough. Use a round cookie cutter to cut out cakes. Transfer cakes to an ungreased cookie sheet and bake for 30 minutes or until cakes just begin to brown. Remove from oven immediately.

—*Loray and Kathleen,* LOUISIANA

Mississippi Fried Pies

The filling for these pies may be made ahead and refrigerated.

Makes 12 Fried Pies

PASTRY:

3 cups flour

1 teaspoon salt

¾ cup vegetable shortening

1 egg, lightly beaten

¼ cup cold water

1 teaspoon white vinegar

FILLING:

3 cups dried apples, peaches, or apricots

1½ cups water

½ cup sugar

¼ teaspoon cinnamon

¼ teaspoon nutmeg

¼ teaspoon ginger

¼ teaspoon allspice

Pastry: In a large bowl, combine flour and salt. Use a pastry cutter or two butter knives to cut in shortening until mixture resembles coarse crumbs. In a small bowl, mix the beaten egg with the water and drizzle over flour mixture. Sprinkle the vinegar into the batter and stir gently until ingredients are well combined. Form the dough into a ball and wrap in plastic wrap. Refrigerate for at least 1 hour.

Filling: Place fruit in a medium saucepan and add water until just covered. Simmer for 20–30 minutes or until fruit is very tender. Add water, if needed, to avoid burning. Drain and allow filling to cool. In a medium bowl, lightly mash fruit, add sugar and spices, and stir to combine. If the filling is refrigerated to use later, warm the fruit slightly in the microwave to make it workable before filling your pies.

(continued on next page)

Divide dough into four equal portions. Cut each portion into three pieces. Roll each piece into a ball. On a lightly floured surface, roll out each ball into a 5- to 6-inch circle. Place 2 heaping tablespoons of filling on one side of each dough round. Use your finger to wet the inside edges of the dough with water, then fold the rounds in half. Crimp the edges of each pie thoroughly to secure the seals. Melt vegetable shortening over medium heat in a large skillet and fry the pies, turning only once, until both sides are golden brown.

—*Nadine and Fred,* MISSISSIPPI

Fried pies are an ingenious combination of tastiness and portability. The pies are made from a circle of pie dough folded in half to create a pocket that is then filled with fruit, often apples or peaches, and deep-fried. Before refrigeration and imports allowed year-round availability of a variety of fruits, many folks would slice and dry fruits to preserve them for consumption in the colder months. Southern lore suggests that fried pies were first produced by slaves and could be tucked into a pocket for a sweet treat in the fields.

Buttermilk Pie

Makes 2 Pies

2 deep-dish pie shells, unbaked
2²/₃ cups sugar
¹/₃ cup flour
4 eggs, well beaten
1¹/₃ sticks (about 5½ ounces) butter, melted

1¹/₃ cups buttermilk
¼ teaspoon vanilla
½ teaspoon lemon extract

Preheat oven to 350°F. Bake the pie shells for 6–7 minutes or just enough to dry them out so they will not be soggy. In a large bowl, mix sugar and flour. Add well-beaten eggs and stir to combine. Add melted butter, buttermilk, vanilla, and lemon extract; mix well. Divide batter evenly between pie shells. Bake for about 45 minutes. Allow the pies to bake until they do not shake in the middle.

—*Topsy*, MISSISSIPPI

Smoky Mountain Mud Pie

Makes 6 to 8 Servings

1¼ stick (⁵/₈ cup) butter
4 tablespoons cocoa powder
1½ teaspoons vanilla
¾ cups self-rising flour

3 eggs, beaten
¾ cup nuts
Vanilla ice cream, for serving
Hot fudge sauce, for serving

Grease a 9-inch pie pan. Melt butter in a large saucepan. Remove from heat and stir in cocoa and vanilla. Add flour, eggs, and nuts; mix well. Pour mixture into pie pan. Place pie in cool oven and set the oven temperature to 325°F. Bake for 40–45 minutes. Pie will not be firmly set. Allow to cool before serving. Top with vanilla ice cream and hot fudge sauce.

—*Mary*, KENTUCKY

Deep Dish Blackberry Pie

Makes 1 Pie

BLACKBERRY FILLING:
3 cups fresh or frozen blackberries,
   thawed and drained
½ cup sugar
2 tablespoons cornstarch
1 teaspoon lemon juice
¼ teaspoon cinnamon

TOPPING:
¾ cup flour
3 teaspoons sugar, divided
¼ teaspoon salt
3 tablespoons butter
1 tablespoon shortening
3 tablespoons cold water
1 egg white, beaten

Blackberry Filling: Preheat oven to 375°F. Grease a 1-quart baking dish. Pour blackberries into a medium bowl. In a separate bowl, add sugar and cornstarch; stir to mix. Sprinkle sugar mixture over berries. Add lemon juice and cinnamon; toss to coat. Spoon filling into baking dish and set aside.

Topping: In a large bowl, combine flour, 1 teaspoon of sugar, and salt. Using two butter knives, cut in butter and shortening until mixture resembles coarse crumbs. Add cold water and mix with a fork until a ball forms. Roll out the dough until ¼-inch thick. Cut dough into ½-inch strips. Weave strips in a lattice pattern on top of the blackberry filling. Crimp the crust edges and brush the crust with egg whites. Sprinkle top of pie with remaining 2 teaspoons sugar.

Bake for 40–45 minutes or until crust is golden brown.

—*Mildred,* VIRGINIA

Apple Butter Pumpkin Pie

Makes 1 Pie

PIE:
1 cup canned solid-pack pumpkin
1 cup apple butter
¼ cup dark brown sugar, packed
½ teaspoon ground cinnamon
¼ teaspoon ground ginger
¼ teaspoon ground nutmeg
¼ teaspoon salt
3 eggs, lightly beaten
1 cup evaporated milk
1 9-inch deep-dish pie shell, unbaked

STREUSEL TOPPING:
3 tablespoons butter, softened
⅓ cup dark brown sugar
½ cup flour
⅓ cup pecans, chopped

Pie: Preheat oven to 375°F. In a large bowl, combine pumpkin and apple butter. Add brown sugar, spices and salt; stir until well combined. Stir in lightly beaten eggs. Add evaporated milk and mix. Pour filling into pie shell and bake for 50–60 minutes.

Streusel: In a small bowl, cream butter and sugar. Add flour and mix until thoroughly combined. Gently mix in pecans.

Top pie with streusel and bake for 15 minutes or until top is golden brown.

—*Rebecca*, TENNESSEE

What moistens the lip and what brightens the eye?
What calls back the past, like the rich Pumpkin pie?

—JOHN GREENLEAF WHITTIER

Sweet Potato Custard Pie

Makes 2 Pies

PIES:

2 pie shells, unbaked

1 cup butter

2 cups sweet potatoes, cooked and mashed

4 eggs, beaten

2 cups sugar

2 tablespoons flour

¼ teaspoon cinnamon

¼ teaspoon nutmeg

⅛ teaspoon mace

1¼ cups milk

1 teaspoon vanilla

1 teaspoon orange extract

TOPPING:

1 cup light brown sugar

1 cup pecans, chopped

½ cup butter

¼ cup flour

Pies: Preheat oven to 325°F. Bake pie shells for 5–7 minutes until they just begin to dry out, but don't brown. Cream butter in a large mixing bowl. Add mashed sweet potatoes to creamed butter and blend. Add beaten eggs and stir to combine. In a separate bowl, mix sugar, flour, cinnamon, nutmeg, and mace. Alternate additions of dry ingredients and milk to the sweet potato mixture. Blend after each addition. Stir in vanilla and orange extract. Divide mixture evenly between the 2 pie shells. Bake 35–40 minutes or until firm.

Topping: Preheat oven to 350°F. In a medium bowl, combine all topping ingredients. Mix well. Spread topping over cooked pies and bake for an additional 15–20 minutes.

—*Lynette,* MISSISSIPPI

Old South Pecan Pie

Makes 1 Pie

CRUST:

1 1/3 cups flour

1 teaspoon sugar

1/2 teaspoon salt

1/3 cup vegetable shortening,
   chilled and cut into pieces

1/2 stick (1/4 cup) unsalted butter,
   chilled and cut into pieces

About 2 tablespoons ice water

FILLING:

2/3 cup sugar

1 cup dark corn syrup

1/3 cup butter, melted

3 eggs, beaten

Dash salt

1 tablespoon cornmeal

1 cup pecans

Crust: In a large bowl, add flour, sugar, and salt; whisk to combine. Using 2 knives or a pasty cutter, cut in butter and shortening until mixture resembles coarse crumbs. Work quickly and DO NOT over-mix. Stir in enough ice water to form moist clumps. Gather clumps into a ball; flatten into a disk. Wrap in plastic and chill for 1 hour.

On a lightly floured surface, roll dough into a 13-inch circle. Transfer to a 9-inch pie pan. Press dough into pan and trim edges. Place in the freezer for 15 minutes.

Preheat oven to 350°F.

Filling: In a large bowl, beat sugar, corn syrup, butter, eggs, salt, and cornmeal. Fold in pecans. Pour filling into piecrust. Bake for 50 minutes or until set and brown. Serve warm.

—*Marg,* SOUTH CAROLINA

Fort Valley Peach Cobbler

Makes 1 Cobbler

1 cup flour
2 cups sugar, divided
2 teaspoons baking powder
Dash salt
1⅛ cups milk
1 stick (½ cup) butter
3 cups fresh peaches, sliced
3 teaspoons pineapple juice
1 teaspoon lemon zest

Preheat oven to 350°F. In a medium bowl, combine flour, 1¼ cups of the sugar, baking powder, salt, and milk; stir until smooth. Place the butter in a 2-quart baking dish and place dish in the oven until the butter has melted. Remove dish from oven and pour the batter on top of the melted butter. Do not stir! In a separate bowl, combine peaches, ¾ cup of the sugar, pineapple juice, and lemon zest. Pour the fruit mixture evenly over the top of the batter. Do not ever stir!! Bake for 1 hour.

—*Becky*, GEORGIA

An apple is an excellent thing—
until you have tried a peach!

—GEORGE DU MAURIER

Apple Brown Betty

Makes 6 to 8 Servings

¾ cup brown sugar, packed
¼ teaspoon cinnamon
¼ teaspoon salt
2 cups breadcrumbs, divided

3 cups apples, sliced
4 tablespoons water
2 tablespoons butter

Preheat oven to 350°F. In a small bowl, combine sugar, cinnamon, and salt. Set aside. Spread 1 cup of the breadcrumbs on the bottom of a 9x13x2-inch baking dish. Cover the breadcrumbs with apples. Sprinkle apples with the sugar mixture. Cover the sugar mixture with the remaining cup of breadcrumbs. Moisten top evenly with water and dot with butter. Bake for 30–40 minutes or until apples are tender.

—*Geraldine*, SOUTH CAROLINA

Cranberry Casserole

This is a great dish to serve during the fall and winter seasons.

Makes 6 to 8 Servings

3 cups apples, chopped
2 cups fresh cranberries
1 cup sugar
½ cup 1-minute oats

½ cup pecans, chopped
½ cup brown sugar
½ cup butter, melted

Preheat oven to 325°F. In a 2-quart casserole dish, mix apples and cranberries. Spread fruit mixture evenly on the bottom of the dish. Sprinkle with the white sugar. Set aside. In a medium bowl, mix oats, pecans, brown sugar, and butter; pour evenly over top of fruit. Cover dish loosely with aluminum foil and bake 45 for minutes. Serve warm.

—*Mary*, ALABAMA

Winter Crisp

You can make a Summer Crisp by replacing the apples and cranberries with 4 cups of fresh peaches and 3 cups of fresh blueberries.

Makes 6 to 8 Servings

FILLING:
½ cup sugar
3 tablespoons flour
1 teaspoon lemon zest
¾ teaspoon lemon juice
5 cups apples, sliced
1 cup cranberries

TOPPING:
²/₃ cup rolled oats
¹/₃ cup brown sugar, packed
¼ cup whole wheat flour
2 teaspoons cinnamon
1 tablespoon butter, melted

Filling: Preheat oven to 375°F. In a medium bowl, combine sugar, flour, and lemon zest. Mix well. Add lemon juice, apples, and cranberries; stir to combine. Spoon filling into a 6-cup baking dish.

Topping: In a small bowl, combine oats, brown sugar, flour, and cinnamon. Stir in melted butter.

Sprinkle topping over the filling. Bake for 30–40 minutes or until filling is bubbly and top is brown. Serve warm or at room temperature.

—*Evelyn,* MISSISSIPPI

Sweet Potato Crunch

Makes 12 Servings

SWEET POTATOES:

3 cups canned sweet potatoes,
    mashed in their own juice

¼ cup milk

¼ cup butter, melted

¾ cup sugar

1 teaspoon vanilla

2 eggs, beaten

1 cup coconut (optional)

CRUNCH TOPPING:

1 cup brown sugar

¼ cup butter, melted

½ cup flour

1 cup pecans, chopped

Sweet Potatoes: Preheat oven to 350°F. Combine all sweet potato ingredients in a large bowl. Mix well. Pour into a well-greased 13x9x2-inch baking dish.

Topping: In a medium bowl, add brown sugar and butter; stir to combine. Gradually add the flour. Mix well. Stir in chopped pecans. Sprinkle topping over potato mixture.

Bake for 35 minutes or until bubbly.

—*Irma*, GEORGIA

Gingerbread with Orange Sauce

Makes 8 to 10 Servings

GINGERBREAD:

2 cups flour	½ cup butter, softened
1 teaspoon baking soda	¾ cup sugar
1 teaspoon ginger	½ cup buttermilk
Dash nutmeg	¾ cup molasses
Dash cinnamon	2 eggs
Dash cloves	

ORANGE SAUCE:

1 cup sugar	1 teaspoon orange zest
Juice of 2 oranges	1 tablespoon butter

Gingerbread: Preheat oven to 350°F. Whisk flour, baking soda, ginger, nutmeg, cinnamon, and cloves in a medium bowl; set aside. In a large bowl, cream butter and sugar. Beat in buttermilk and molasses. Beat in eggs, one at a time. Mix each egg into ingredients thoroughly before adding the next. Pour batter into 9x13x2-inch pan. Bake for 30 minutes, or until center of gingerbread is set.

Orange Sauce: Combine the sugar, orange juice, and zest in a medium saucepan. Boil over medium-high heat for about 10 minutes. When the sauce becomes thick, remove it from the heat and stir in the butter.

Smother gingerbread with orange sauce and serve warm.

—*In memory of Esther,* ARKANSAS

Had I but a penny in the world, thou shouldst have it for gingerbread.

—WILLIAM SHAKESPEARE

Apple Dumplings

Makes 12 Dumplings

SYRUP:
2 cups sugar
2 cups water

DUMPLINGS:
2 cups flour
2 teaspoons baking powder
1 teaspoon salt
$^2/_3$ cup shortening
½ cup milk
3–4 apples, peeled and sliced
¼ teaspoon cinnamon
¼ teaspoon nutmeg
4 tablespoons butter

Syrup: Combine sugar and water in a saucepan; bring to a boil. Reduce heat and let simmer while preparing apples and dough.

Dumplings: Preheat oven to 375°F. In a large bowl, sift flour with baking powder and salt. Cut in shortening. Add milk and stir until batter is moistened. Prepare a lightly floured surface and roll out dough until ¼-inch thick. Cut dough into 6-inch squares. Divide apples evenly and arrange in center of squares. Sprinkle with cinnamon and nutmeg. Dot with butter. Fold four corners of dough so they meet in the center and firmly pinch edges to seal. Place dumplings in baking dish and smother with syrup. Bake for 35 minutes.

—*Pauline*, NORTH CAROLINA

Alabama "Blue Ribbon" Banana Pudding

During the summer of 1997 at our Annual Congressional Family Picnic, each spouse was asked to bring a dessert with a hint of her state. To my surprise, I won 1st place for my Alabama Banana Pudding. I was crowned with a chef's hat and my scepter was a wooden spoon. I'd like to add that my court, the second- through fourth-place winners, were all Southern Spouses!

Makes 8 Servings

PUDDING:

¾ cup sugar	3 egg yolks, beaten
Dash salt	2 cups half & half
¼ cup flour	2–4 bananas, sliced
1 tablespoon vanilla	15 vanilla wafers

MERINGUE:

3 egg whites	6 tablespoons sugar
2 dashes cream of tartar	½ teaspoon vanilla

Pudding: Combine sugar, salt, and flour in a large bowl. Stir in vanilla and egg yolks. Transfer mixture to a double boiler and heat while slowly stirring in half & half. Continue to stir frequently. Remove from heat when the pudding has thickened.

Meringue: In a separate bowl, combine egg whites and cream of tartar; beat for 2 minutes. Slowly add sugar and vanilla. Continue to beat mixture until egg whites form very stiff peaks.

Preheat oven to 350°F. Layer wafers and banana slices in a 1½ quart baking dish. Cover with pudding. Top with meringue. Bake until meringue turns golden brown, about 12–15 minutes.

—*Patsy*, ALABAMA

Bread Pudding with Lemon Sauce

Makes 6 Servings

BREAD PUDDING:

5 eggs, beaten

1 cup sugar

2 cups milk

1½ teaspoons vanilla

¼ teaspoon nutmeg

¼ cup butter, melted

5 slices day-old white or French bread,
   crusts removed, cubed

½ cup raisins (optional)

LEMON SAUCE:

1 cup sugar

1 tablespoon cornstarch

½ teaspoon salt

3 eggs, lightly beaten

Juice and zest from 2 lemons

1 cup water

2 tablespoons butter

Bread pudding: Preheat oven to 350°F. In a large bowl, add eggs, sugar, milk, vanilla, and nutmeg; stir until well combined. Stir in melted butter. Add cubed bread and raisins; mix well. Pour into a greased 2-quart casserole dish and bake for 45 minutes.

Lemon sauce: Mix sugar, cornstarch, and salt in the top of a double boiler. Add eggs, lemon juice, lemon zest, and water. Mix well. Cook over simmering heat until thick, stirring constantly. Add butter and cool.

Pour lemon sauce over warm bread pudding just before serving.

—*Grace*, ARKANSAS

Persimmon Pudding

Makes 9 to 12 Servings

Several ripe persimmons, enough to make 2 cups of persimmon pulp
½ cup butter
3 eggs, beaten

2 cups sugar
2 cups milk
2 cups self-rising flour
1 teaspoon vanilla
1 teaspoon cinnamon

Preheat oven to 350°F. Remove the skins and seeds from the persimmons and purée the pulp in a blender; set aside. Melt the butter in a 9x13x2-inch baking dish. In a large bowl, add beaten eggs and sugar; stir to combine. Alternate additions of milk and flour; mix well between each addition. Add vanilla, cinnamon, and persimmon pulp; stir until thoroughly combined. Pour batter into the buttery baking dish and bake for 1 hour or until a knife inserted in the center comes out clean. Serve warm.

—*Pauline,* NORTH CAROLINA

Biscuit Pudding

Makes 8 to 10 Servings

2 eggs, beaten
2 cups milk
1 cup sugar
½ teaspoon vanilla

1 teaspoon ground cinnamon
¼ teaspoon ground nutmeg
3 cups biscuits, crumbled

Preheat oven tp 350°F. In a large bowl, mix the beaten eggs, milk, sugar, vanilla, cinnamon, and nutmeg. Add the crumbled biscuits and stir until well combined. Spoon the mixture into a lightly greased 2-quart casserole dish. Bake 20–25 minutes or until a knife inserted in the center comes out clean.

—*Sarah,* ALABAMA

Crybabies

For a Crowd

Makes 10 Dozen Cookies

3 sticks (1½ cups) butter

2 cups sugar, plus more for coating cookies

2 eggs, beaten

½ cup molasses

4 cups flour, sifted

4 teaspoons baking soda

2 teaspoons ginger

2 teaspoons cinnamon

2 teaspoons salt

Preheat oven to 325°F. Grease cookie sheets. In a large bowl, cream butter and sugar. Add beaten eggs and molasses; stir to combine. Sift dry ingredients into a separate bowl. Gradually mix dry ingredients into wet ingredients until thoroughly blended. Cover bowl and refrigerate for at least 1 hour. Roll dough into ¾-inch balls. Roll the balls in sugar. Place on cookie sheets and bake for 10–12 minutes.

—*Gail,* ARKANSAS

Benne Seed Cookies

Makes 6 Dozen Cookies

½ cup benne (sesame) seeds, toasted
1 stick (½ cup) butter
1 cup sugar
1 egg, beaten
1½ cups self-rising flour
1 teaspoon vanilla

Preheat oven to 350°F. Spread Benne seeds in a baking pan and bake them until they pop. In a large bowl, cream butter and sugar; add egg, flour, and vanilla; mix. Stir in baked Benne seeds. Drop teaspoons of batter onto cookie sheets. Flatten each cookie with a fork dampened in water. Bake for about 15 minutes or until light brown.

—*Addie*, SOUTH CAROLINA

Nutty Beehives

My father-in-law keeps bees.
This is one of the honey cookie recipes I made up using his honey.

Makes 15 to 20 Cookies

1 stick (½ cup) butter	¼ cup powdered sugar
½ cup honey, (preferably	2 cups flour
raw, local wildflower honey)	½ cup pecans, ground
1 teaspoon vanilla	Powdered sugar, for dusting

Cream butter, honey, vanilla, and powdered sugar in a large bowl. Gently blend in flour and ground pecans. Chill, covered, for 1 hour or more. Preheat oven to 350°F. Roll the dough into balls or shape into beehives and place on an ungreased cookie sheet. Bake 10–12 minutes. Remove immediately from cookie sheet and place on absorbent paper towels for a few minutes. Transfer to a wire rack and cool completely. Dust with powdered sugar, if desired.

—*Sylvia*, LOUISIANA

Rocks

Makes 4 Dozen Cookies

1½ cups sugar
1 cup butter
3 eggs
3 cups flour
¼ teaspoon salt
1 teaspoon baking soda
½ cup warm water
1 teaspoon cinnamon
2 teaspoons allspice
1 teaspoon ground cloves
1 pound nuts, chopped
1 pound raisins or chopped dates

Preheat oven to 350°F. Cream sugar and butter in a large bowl. Add eggs one at a time, stirring after each addition. In a separate bowl, sift flour with salt. Add to the creamed butter mixture and stir to combine. Dissolve baking soda in warm water and add to the batter. Stir in cinnamon, allspice, and cloves. Gently stir in nuts and fruit. Drop batter by teaspoonsful onto an ungreased baking sheet. Bake for 10–15 minutes or until set and browned. Do not overcook.

—*In memory of Leila,* ARKANSAS

Peanut Blossom Cookies

Makes 24 Cookies

¾ cup creamy peanut butter
½ cup butter, softened
⅓ cup sugar
⅓ cup brown sugar, packed
1 egg
2 tablespoons milk
1 teaspoon vanilla
1½ cups flour
1 teaspoon baking soda
½ teaspoon salt
Sugar, for coating
48 Hershey's kisses,
    wrappers removed and kisses frozen

Preheat oven to 375°F. In a large bowl, cream peanut butter and butter. Add sugar and brown sugar; beat until fluffy. Add egg, milk, and vanilla; beat well. In a separate bowl, sift flour with baking soda and salt. Gradually stir flour mixture into peanut butter mixture. Shape dough into 1-inch balls. Roll balls in sugar and place on ungreased cookie sheets. Bake for 8–10 minutes or until light brown. Remove from oven and immediately place one kiss in the center of each cookie. Press kiss down gently until the cookie cracks slightly around the edges. Cool on wire racks.

—*Marie,* TENNESSEE

A peanut is not a nut! It is actually an odd bean in the legume family and grows on a bush that develops its pods underground. Georgia produces almost half of the total U. S. peanut crop, and every American eats on the average of three pounds of peanuts annually. Indulge in the Peanut Blossoms featured in the recipe on this page. It is an excellent way to reach your quota of peanut consumption for the year.

Grandma's Lace Cookies

Makes 4 to 5 Dozen Cookies *For a Crowd*

1 cup old-fashioned oats
1 cup sugar
2 tablespoons plus 1 teaspoon flour
¼ teaspoon salt
1 egg, lightly beaten
½ cup butter, melted
2 teaspoons vanilla

Preheat oven to 350°F. Line 2 cookie sheets with aluminum foil. In a large bowl, combine oats, sugar, flour, and salt. Mix well. Add lightly beaten egg, butter, and vanilla. Stir to thoroughly combine. Drop by ½ teaspoonfuls 3 inches apart on cookie sheets. Bake for 6–8 minutes or until edges are slightly brown. Cool completely before removing from foil.

—Becky, ALABAMA

Seven Steps to Heaven

Makes 12 Bars

1 stick (½ cup) butter, melted
1 cup graham cracker crumbs
1 (14-ounce) can sweetened condensed milk
1 cup pecans, chopped
6 ounces shredded coconut
6 ounces chocolate chips
6 ounces peanut butter chips

Preheat oven to 350°F. In a small bowl, mix melted butter and graham cracker crumbs. Press mixture onto the bottom of a 9x13-inch baking pan. Cover crumbs with condensed milk, and layer with pecans, coconut, chocolate chips, and peanut butter chips. Bake for 30 minutes. Allow to cool completely before cutting into squares.

—Betty, VIRGINIA

Melt-in-Your-Mouth Blueberry Bars

Blueberry bars may be made in advance and frozen.

Makes 9 to 12 Bars

BLUEBERRY BARS:
½ cup butter
¾ cup sugar
2 eggs
1 teaspoon vanilla
¾ cup milk
1½ cups self-rising flour
½ cup rolled oats
¼ teaspoon cinnamon
1½ cups fresh blueberries
¼ cup brown sugar, packed

TOPPING:
1 cup powdered sugar
3–4 tablespoons milk

Blueberry Bars: Preheat oven to 325°F. In a large bowl, cream butter and sugar. Add eggs and beat well. Add vanilla and milk; stir to combine. In a separate bowl, mix flour, oats, and cinnamon. Add blueberries to flour mixture and toss gently to coat. Fold the blueberry mixture into the batter. Pour batter into a greased 9x9-inch square baking dish. Sprinkle batter with brown sugar. Bake for 30–40 minutes or until golden brown. Allow to cool.

Topping: In a small bowl, whisk sugar and milk until smooth.

Drizzle topping on cooled bars.

—*Brenda,* NORTH CAROLINA

Southern-Style Pecan Fudge

Makes 15 Squares of Fudge

3¾ cups powdered sugar
6 tablespoons butter
½ cup unsweetened
   cocoa powder

¼ cup milk
1 tablespoon vanilla
¼ teaspoon salt
1 cup pecans, chopped

Butter a 9x5-inch baking pan. In a saucepan over low heat, add sugar, butter, cocoa, milk, vanilla, and salt, stirring constantly until smooth. Remove from heat, stir in nuts, and quickly spread mixture into greased pan. Cool and cut into squares.

—Roscoe, NORTH CAROLINA

Grandma Jones Pecan Pringles

Makes 3 Dozen Pringles

²/₃ cup light brown sugar, packed
½ stick (¼ cup) butter
½ cup chocolate chips

1 egg
1 teaspoon vanilla
1 cup pecans, finely chopped

Preheat oven to 350°F. Line 2 cookie sheets with greased aluminum foil. Combine brown sugar and butter in a saucepan. Cook over low heat, stirring until butter is melted. Add chocolate chips and continue to stir. When chocolate is melted, remove from heat, and allow to cool slightly. Whisk in egg and vanilla. Stir in nuts. Drop a full teaspoon of dough for each cookie onto cookie sheets, about 2 inches apart. Cook about 8 minutes. Do not over-bake. These cookies are easy to burn. Gently remove from foil and place in refrigerator until cooled.

—Mary, NORTH CAROLINA

Creamy Pralines

Makes 4 Dozen Pralines

3 cups sugar	1 teaspoon baking soda
1 cup buttermilk	1 teaspoon vanilla
¼ cup light corn syrup	4 cups pecans
Pinch salt	

In a large pan, combine sugar, buttermilk, corn syrup, and salt. Bring to a boil and add baking soda. Mixture will foam when baking soda is added. Stir and cook until mixture forms a soft ball when dropped into water or registers 149°F on a candy thermometer. Remove from heat and add vanilla. Beat until the candy thickens and loses its gloss. Stir in pecans. Drop candy by teaspoonfuls onto a greased cookie sheet. Cool completely.

—*Geraldine,* SOUTH CAROLINA

Easy Pralines

Makes 2 Dozen Pralines

1 (3.5-ounce) box cook and serve butterscotch pudding
1 cup sugar
1 cup brown sugar
½ cup evaporated milk
1 tablespoon butter
½–¾ cup pecans, halves and pieces

Combine pudding mix, sugar, brown sugar, evaporated milk, and butter in a saucepan. Cook over low heat, stirring until sugar dissolves and mixture comes to a boil. Continue to boil gently, stirring often, until a small amount of mixture dropped in cold water forms a soft ball (230°F on a candy thermometer). Remove from heat. Add pecans and beat until candy starts to lose its gloss, about 3–5 minutes. Drop by tablespoonfuls onto waxed paper. Cool completely until firm. Store in an airtight container.

—*Donna,* SOUTH CAROLINA

Fresh Peach Ice Cream

*Strawberries or bananas may be substituted
for the peaches in this recipe.*

Makes 1 Gallon of Ice Cream

6 whole eggs
1–2 cups sugar, to taste
1 (14-ounce) can sweetened condensed milk
½ teaspoon vanilla
4 cups whole milk
2 cups half & half
8–10 ripe peaches, peeled and mashed

In a large bowl, whisk eggs until they're as thick as custard.
Gradually whisk in the sugar. Whisk in condensed milk and the
vanilla. Add the whole milk and half & half and blend. Pour
mixture into an ice cream freezer and follow the manufacturer's
directions. Add the peaches when the ice cream is half frozen and
then let the freezing process continue.

—*Wilma*, KENTUCKY

Lime Sorbet

*You can replace the lime juice with any flavoring you wish—almond,
vanilla, guava. Italian soda syrups also work great!*

Makes 1 Cup

⅓ cup sugar   1 lime, juiced
⅔ cup water   1 pinch salt

Place a one-quart freezer safe bowl in the freezer. Combine sugar
and water in a small saucepan. Stir over medium heat until sugar
dissolves. Bring mixture to a boil, reduce heat, and simmer for 6
minutes. Remove from heat and let cool. When cool, stir in lime
juice and salt. Pour into the chilled bowl. Place in the freezer and
freeze, whisking every 20 to 30 minutes until mixture is almost
firm. Serve in chilled dishes.

—*Teesha*, MISSISSIPPI

Beverages

> *Nothing would be more tiresome*
> *than eating and drinking*
> *if God had not made them*
> *a pleasure as well as a necessity.*

—Voltaire

Hot Caramel Chocolate

Makes 6 Servings

1/3 cup sugar
1/3 cup unsweetened cocoa powder
1/3 cup water
6 milk chocolate caramel squares
6 cups milk
Whipped cream, to taste

In a large saucepan, combine sugar, cocoa powder, and water. Cook over medium heat, stirring, until sugar is dissolved. Add chocolate caramels and stir until candies are melted. Stir in milk and heat until steaming. Pour into mugs. Serve hot with whipped cream.

—*Debbie,* NORTH CAROLINA

Mulled Cider

Makes 1 Gallon

1 gallon apple cider
1/4 cup honey or brown sugar
3 tablespoons cloves
1 tablespoon ground cinnamon
1 tablespoon lemon juice

Mix all ingredients in a big pot and simmer for 20 minutes. Serve hot on a cold winter day.

—*In loving memory of Wanda,* ARKANSAS

Mint Tea

Makes 4 Cups

12–15 (4-inch) fresh mint sprigs,
   coarsely chopped
Boiling water to fill teapot
Honey, to taste

Place mint in a teapot. Pour the boiling water over the mint. Let stand ten minutes. Sweeten with honey.

—*Delores*, ARKANSAS

If you are cold, tea will warm you—
if you are too heated, it will cool you—
if you are depressed, it will cheer you—
if you are excited, it will calm you.

—WILLIAM GLADSTONE

Russian Tea

Makes 8 Cups

6 cups water, divided
2 tablespoons loose black tea
1 cup sugar
12 cloves
Juice of 3 large oranges
Juice of 3 lemons
½ cup pineapple juice

In a saucepan, boil 4 cups of water. Pour boiling water over tea in a tempered glass container and let steep for 10 minutes. Strain. In a saucepan, add 2 cups of water, sugar, and cloves; bring to a boil. Combine the tea and the sugar/clove mixture. Add the juices. Strain twice and serve hot.

—*Laura,* NORTH CAROLINA

Tea for Cough

It really works!

Makes 1 Cup

1 cup hot water
1 tablespoon thyme, fresh or ground
1 tablespoon honey

Add thyme and honey to hot water. Cool. Take a teaspoon every hour.

—*Betty,* ARKANSAS

Cappuccino Cooler

Makes 1 Cooler

½ cup cold coffee
½ cup chocolate ice cream
⅛ cup chocolate syrup
½ cup crushed ice
Whipped cream, to taste

In a blender, combine coffee, chocolate ice cream, and chocolate syrup. Blend until smooth. Pour over crushed ice and top with a dollop of whipped cream.

—*Marlene*, LOUISIANA

Coffee Punch  *For a Crowd*

Makes 2¾ Gallons

1 gallon strong coffee, room temperature
2–3 quarts milk
1 gallon vanilla ice cream
Sugar, to taste

Pour coffee and milk into a punch bowl. Add ice cream by the spoonful, add sugar to taste, and serve.

—*Marcia*, ALABAMA

Florence's Southern Punch Mix

Makes 5 Cups of Mix or 10 Servings

2 cups sugar
2½ cups water
Juice of 6 lemons
Zest of 2 lemons
Juice of 2 oranges

Zest of 1 orange
½ cup fresh mint, crushed
5 cups ginger ale
Orange slices or frosted grapes,
    for garnish

Combine sugar and water in a pot and bring to a boil. Boil 5 minutes or until sugar is dissolved. In a medium bowl, combine lemon juice and zest, orange juice and zest, and mint. Pour sugar/water mixture over juices, zest, and mint; cover and let stand for 1 hour. Strain and chill. To serve, mix equal parts punch mix and ginger ale; pour over ice. Garnish with orange slices or frosted grapes.

—*Frances*, ARKANSAS

Peppermint Punch

For a Crowd

Makes 20 Cups of Punch

2 quarts cold milk
2 quarts ginger ale
1 quart peppermint ice cream
Peppermint stick candy, crushed, for garnish

In a punch bowl, combine milk and ginger ale. Place scoops of ice cream on top of the punch. Garnish with crushed peppermint sticks.

—*Ophie*, TENNESSEE

Root Beer

Makes 1 (2-liter) Bottle or 8 Cups

1 cup sugar
¼ teaspoon active dry yeast
1¼ teaspoons root beer concentrate
7¼ cups water

Wash and dry a 2-liter bottle with a tight-fitting cap. Bottle and cap must be VERY clean and dry. Use a funnel to pour sugar and yeast into bottle. Cap and shake well. Use funnel to pour root beer extract and half of the water into the bottle. Remove funnel and swirl liquid in bottle until yeast is dissolved. Add rest of water and cap tightly. Let sit at room temperature for 2 days, then refrigerate. Root beer is ready to drink in 3–4 days.

—*Pat*, TENNESSEE

Dazzling Lemonade

Makes 2 Quarts

1 cup sugar
½ cup water
1¼ cups fresh lemon juice (juice of 8 lemons)
1 cup fresh raspberries
1 pint pineapple sherbet
3 cups carbonated water, chilled

Bring sugar and water to a boil in a small saucepan, stirring occasionally. Cook for 2 minutes or until sugar dissolves; remove from heat. Allow to cool completely. In a glass bowl, combine cooled syrup, lemon juice, and raspberries; cover and chill for 2 hours. Just before serving, scoop sherbet into punch bowl. Combine juice mixture and chilled, carbonated water and pour over sherbet.

—*Jill*, ALABAMA

Strawberry Smoothie

Makes 1 Smoothie

1 cup milk
¼ cup powdered sugar
8–10 strawberries, fresh or frozen

In a blender, add milk and sugar; blend on high speed. Add the strawberries one at a time and blend until desired consistency.

—*Micah*, ARKANSAS

Banana Smoothie

Makes 1 Smoothie

½ cup milk   1 tablespoon honey
½ banana   Dash vanilla

In a blender, combine all ingredients and blend until thick and foamy. Pour into a tumbler or a mug.

—*Muriel*, NORTH CAROLINA

Cantaloupe Shake

Makes 1 Shake

½ cup vanilla ice cream
½ cup cantaloupe, chopped
½ cup milk

Place all ingredients in a blender and blend until smooth.

—*Lonnie*, ARKANSAS

Banana Eggnog

This eggnog is a great use for overripe bananas! When I have overripe bananas, I peel them, package two in a sandwich bag, and put them in the freezer. This drink is also delicious without the eggs.

Makes 1 Serving

1 ripe banana, frozen
½ teaspoon sugar, or more to taste
1 teaspoon vanilla
1 egg
1 cup cold milk
Nutmeg, to taste

Place all ingredients in a blender and purée. Pour into a glass and sprinkle with nutmeg.

—*Josie*, ALABAMA

Peanut Butter Fruit Shake

Makes 4 Shakes

2 cups strawberries, stems removed, quartered
1 banana, sliced
1 cup milk
¾ cup plain yogurt
¼ cup creamy peanut butter

Place all ingredients in a blender. Blend until smooth and serve.

—*Mary*, NORTH CAROLINA

Virgin Mary

Makes 1 Serving

6 ounces tomato juice
3 tablespoons beef or vegetable broth
3 teaspoons lemon juice
¼ teaspoon Worcestershire sauce
Dash Tabasco, or more to taste
Dash salt (optional)
Lemon slices, for garnish
Celery sticks, for garnish

Mix all ingredients well and chill. Serve in an "old fashioned" glass or short tumbler over ice cubes. Garnish with a slice of lemon, a celery stick "swizzle," and a grind of fresh pepper. Add an ounce of vodka to make it a Bloody Mary, or, if you're using beef stock, a Bloody Bull.

—*Sue*, LOUISIANA

Tomato Cooler

Makes 1 Tomato Cooler

½ cup tomato juice
½ cup buttermilk
Juice from ¼ lemon (¾ tablespoon)
Dash dill seed
Dash seasoned salt
Dash garlic salt
Dash onion salt
Green onion, for garnish

Mix all ingredients and pour into a glass over crushed ice. Use a stalk of green onion as a swizzle stick.

—*Ophie*, TENNESSEE

Peachy Pleasure

Peeling a peach is easy as punch! Just make a shallow "X" at the bottom of the peach, and submerge it in rapidly boiling water for about 20 seconds. Then, plunge the peach into cold water. The peel should come off in big, easy strips.

Makes 12 to 14 Servings

4 fresh peaches, peeled, pitted, and quartered
½ cup superfine sugar
½ cup peach liqueur or brandy
3 (750 ml) bottles champagne
1 liter club soda
Mint leaves, for garnish
Additional fresh peach slices, for garnish

Combine peaches, sugar, and liqueur in a blender. Process until smooth. Pour into a punch bowl. Slowly pour the champagne and club soda over the peach mixture and stir gently. Garnish with mint leaves and fresh peach slices.

—*Jeanette*, SOUTH CAROLINA

Peach Fuzz

If peaches are not in season, let the peaches soak in some lemon juice and sugar for 15 minutes to spark up the flavor.

Makes 3 Servings

1 (6-ounce) can lemonade concentrate (Pink is pretty!)
6 ounces vodka
3 peaches, quartered and pitted

Pour all ingredients into a blender. Fill to the top with ice. Blend on high for 20 seconds or until the consistency is slushy.

—*Anne*, ALABAMA

Yellow Bird

To make simple syrup, combine 2 parts sugar and 1 part water in a saucepan. Bring to a boil and cook until sugar dissolves.

Makes 1 Serving

1 ounce light rum
2 tablespoons lemon juice
½ ounce banana liqueur
½ ounce apricot brandy

3 teaspoons simple syrup
3 tablespoons orange juice
3 tablespoons pineapple juice

Mix all ingredients well. Pour in glass over ice.

—*Kathleen and Rhonda,* LOUISIANA

Eggnog  *For a Crowd*

Makes 24 Servings

12 large eggs, separated
4 cups bourbon
1½ cups superfine sugar, divided
1 pint whipping cream
Nutmeg, grated, to taste, for garnish
Toasted, salted pecans, for serving

Beat egg whites in a large bowl until they just form stiff peaks, but are still creamy. Set aside. In another large bowl, beat egg yolks until creamy and light. Whisk in bourbon and ¾ cup of the sugar. Set aside. Whip the cream and the remaining ¾ cup of sugar in a separate bowl until very soft peaks form. Pour the whipping cream/ sugar mixture into the egg yolks. Gently fold the egg whites into the egg yolk mixture. Top each serving with grated nutmeg. Serve immediately with toasted, salted pecans.

—*Janis,* ALABAMA
In loving memory of Park

Brandy Alexander

Makes 1 Serving

2 cups vanilla ice cream
1 ounce brandy
1 ounce crème de cacao
Shaved chocolate, for topping

In a blender, add ice cream, brandy, and crème de cacao. Blend until smooth. Pour into glass and top with shaved chocolate.

—*Mary,* ALABAMA

Christmas Punch

Similar to Sangria; good anytime! You can make this punch a day or two ahead of time and store it in the refrigerator, but don't add the club soda and garnishes until serving time.

Makes 1 Gallon

1 cup brandy
1 cup sugar
½ gallon dry red wine
1 (6-ounce) can frozen orange juice concentrate
Juice of 6 lemons
1 quart club soda
Cherries, for garnish
Lemon, lime, or orange slices, for garnish

In a small saucepan, add the brandy and warm over low heat. Add sugar and stir until dissolved. Remove from heat. Add wine, orange juice, and lemon juice. Refrigerate until chilled.

Pour mixture into punch bowl and add chilled club soda. Garnish with cherries, lemon, lime, or orange slices.

—*Anne,* ALABAMA

Mint Julep Mix

Makes 3 Cups of Mix or 16 Servings

2 cups sugar
2 cups water
3 cups fresh mint leaves, packed
Fresh mint sprigs, for garnish
Bourbon, to taste, for serving

Bring sugar and water to a boil in a small saucepan, stirring occasionally. Cook for 2 minutes or until sugar dissolves; remove from heat. Place mint into a sealable 1-quart jar. Pour sugar water into the jar. Cap and refrigerate for at least 12 hours before serving. Will keep for up to 2 weeks. To serve, combine equal parts bourbon and mint julep mix; pour into glasses over ice. Garnish with a sprig of fresh mint in each glass.

—*Suzie Rae*, KENTUCKY

Wassail  For a Crowd

Makes 5 Gallons

6 quarts water
7 cups sugar
1 tablespoon whole cloves
15 cinnamon sticks
2 (12-ounce) cans frozen lemonade concentrate
4 (12-ounce) cans frozen orange juice concentrate
3 gallons apple cider
1½ liters (fifths) light rum

Combine water and sugar in a large kettle. Place cloves and cinnamon in a cheesecloth bag and tie it to the inside edge of the kettle. Slowly bring water to a boil and boil for 10 minutes. Cover and let stand for 1 hour. Strain. Add lemonade, orange juice, and cider. Heat, but do not let mixture simmer or boil. Add rum and serve hot.

—*Reverend Denis*, ALABAMA

Acknowledgments

The folks at 3D Press would like to extend a sincere thank you to each recipe contributor without whose generosity this cookbook would not have been possible. And a special thank you is extended to the people at the following churches and Christian organizations who graciously offered their cookbooks for use in this project.

ALABAMA
Bethel Baptist Church
2291 County Road 31
Newton, AL 36352

First United Methodist Church
120 West 2nd Street
Bay Minette, AL 36507

St. Thomas Episcopal Church
210 Church Street
Greenville, AL 36037

ARKANSAS
First Presbyterian Church
717 West 32ndAvenue
Pine Bluff, AR 71603

St. Mary's Catholic Church
5118 St. Mary's Lane
Altus, AR 72821

Taylor United Methodist Church
406 Long Avenue—Highway 132
Taylor, AR 71861

Temple Baptist Church
1812 South Dixieland Road
Rogers, AR 72758

GEORGIA
Clinch Chapel United
Methodist Church
165 Owens Ferry Road
Woodbine, GA 31569

First Salem Baptist Church
191 Twin Church Road
Montezuma, Georgia 3106

Macedonia Baptist Church
1948 Gladstone Street
Savannah, Georgia 31406

KENTUCKY
Beech Fork Community Center
2749 Highway 421
Helton, KY 40840

Bethel Holiness Church
122 Bethel Church Road
Melber, KY 42069

First Baptist Church
901 Ashland Drive
Russell, KY 41169

First United Methodist Church
1632 Cumberland Falls Highway
Corbin, KY 40701

LOUISIANA
Albany Hungarian
Presbyterian Church
Hungarian Presbyterian Church Road
Hammond, LA 70403

Oakmont Church of God
5925 W. 70th Street
Shreveport, LA 71129

St. Peter's Catholic Church
4702 Highway 451
Bordelonville, LA 71320

Unitarian Church of Baton Rouge
8470 Goodwood Blvd.
Baton Rouge, LA 70806

MISSISSIPPI
First Baptist Church
108 East Lampkin Street
Starkville, MS 39759

First Baptist Church of Brandon
309 South College Street
Brandon, MS 39042

Ford's Creek Baptist Church
2758 Fords Creek Road
Poplarville, MS 39470

NORTH CAROLINA
Christ the King Catholic Church
714 Stone Street
Kings Mountain, NC 28086

Faith Lighthouse Holiness Church
925 Purvis Road
Rowland, NC 28383

Good Shepherd Moravian Church
1474 Kerner Road
Kernersville, NC 27284

Hickory Grove Presbyterian Church
5735 East W. T. Harris Boulevard
Charlotte, NC 28215

New Life Church of Christ
539 Becker Drive
Roanoke Rapids, NC 27870

River of Life Church
3101 Blue Ridge Road
Raleigh, NC 27612

Thomasville First Pentecostal
Holiness Church
509 Cloniger Drive
Thomasville, NC 27360

Warlick's Baptist Church
2684 Warlick's Church Road
Connelly Springs, NC 28612

SOUTH CAROLINA
Pacolet Mills Baptist Church
385 Stone Street
Pacolet Mills, SC 29373

St. Matthews Lutheran Church
405 King Street
Charleston, SC 29403

TENNESSEE
First United Methodist Church
27 East Church Street
Lexington, TN 38351

Franklin Community Church
830 Countrywood Drive
Franklin, TN 37064

Hillcrest Baptist Church
3504 Laws Chapel Road
Maryville, TN 37803

VIRGINIA
McCutchen Presbyterian Church
1180 Longhollow Road
Buena Vista, VA 24416

Missionettes/Royal Rangers
410 Ash Street
Honaker, VA 24260

Trinity United Methodist Church
409 Arnett Boulevard
Danville, VA 24540

Availability of the individual church and Christian organization cookbooks will vary.
Purchase information may be obtained by contacting the church or organization directly.

Recipe Index

Also Available from 3D Press

High Altitude Baking
$14.95 / 192 pages / ISBN 978-1-889593-15-9

The Bed & Breakfast Cookbook Series

New England Bed & Breakfast Cookbook
(CT, MA, ME, NH, RI, & VT)
$19.95 / 320 pages / ISBN 978-1-889593-12-8

North Carolina Bed & Breakfast Cookbook
$19.95 / 320 pages / ISBN 978-1-889593-08-1

Pennsylvania Bed & Breakfast Cookbook
$19.95 / 304 pages / ISBN 978-1-889593-18-0

Virginia Bed & Breakfast Cookbook
$19.95 / 320 pages / ISBN 978-1-889593-14-2

Washington State Bed & Breakfast Cookbook
$19.95 / 320 pages / ISBN 978-1-889593-05-0

New Titles in Spring and Summer 2008

Georgia Bed & Breakfast Cookbook
$19.95 / 320 pages / ISBN 978-1-889593-19-7

Texas Bed & Breakfast Cookbook
revised and updated
$19.95 / 320 pages / ISBN 978-1-889593-20-3

California Bed and Breakfast Cookbook
revised and updated
$19.95 / 328 pages / ISBN 978-1-889593-21-0

3D Press Order Form

3005 Center Green Drive   Suite 220 · Boulder CO 80301
800-258-5830 · www.bigearthpublishing.com

Please Send Me	Price	Quantity
Southern Church Suppers	$19.95	_____
High Altitude Baking	$14.95	_____
California Bed & Breakfast Cookbook *(available Summer 2008)*	$19.95	_____
Georgia Bed & Breakfast Cookbook *(available Summer 2008)*	$19.95	_____
New England Bed & Breakfast Cookbook	$19.95	_____
North Carolina Bed & Breakfast Cookbook	$19.95	_____
Pennsylvania Bed & Breakfast Cookbook	$19.95	_____
Texas Bed & Breakfast Cookbook *(available Spring 2008)*	$19.95	_____
Virginia Bed & Breakfast Cookbook	$19.95	_____
Washington State Bed & Breakfast Cookbook	$19.95	_____

Subtotal $ _____

Add $5.00 shipping for 1st book add $1 for each additional book **$** _____

Total Enclosed $ _____

Send To

Name _____

Address _____

City /State/Zip _____

Phone _____ Gift from _____

We accept checks and money orders. Please make checks payable to Big Earth Publishing.

Please charge my   **VISA**   **MASTERCARD**   **AMEX**   **DISCOVER**
(circle one)

Card Number _____

Expiration Date _____